THE CUSTOMS DICTIONARY

M000223700

THE CUSTOMER EXPERIENCE DICTIONARY

1st edition

EVERYTHING YOU EVER WANTED TO KNOW ABOUT CX

by
BEN PHILLIPS

PUBLISHING

Published by Rockstar CX Publishing
United Kingdom
www.rockstarcxpublishing.com

First published in December 2020

ISBN 978-1-9163120-1-2

Quantity sales. Special discounts are available on quantity
purchases by corporations, associations, and others. For details,
contact publishing@rockstar.cx

This book is dedicated to my family...

Susannah, Lyndon, Ashton, Miles and Jax.

FOREWORD

Hi. My name is James Dodkins and my company Rockstar CX, among other things, publishes un-boring business books.

Which is why when Ben approached me about publishing a dictionary about CX, I wasn't certain how it would turn out or that it would be un-boring. What I was sure of, however, is that it was needed.

In preparation for writing this foreword, I started thinking about just why the CX community so desperately needs a CX Dictionary. I came to the following conclusion:

One of the best things about CX is that it is one of the most thought-diverse disciplines in the world.

One of the worst things about CX is that it is one of the most thought-diverse disciplines in the world.

This is a paradox. And what is clear from this paradox is that there is no one way to "do" CX. Different professionals, companies and thought leaders are regularly creating new ways to be different, better and diverse at CX. That is both a good thing and a bad thing at the same time.

Many people are drawn to CX because there are always new things to learn, new techniques to master and new ideas to validate. There are new personalities to follow, new research to analyse and new approaches to attempt. There is new technology to evaluate and new assumptions to test. CX never stands still.

Many people are driven from CX for the very same reasons.

While I don't have the answer to this paradox, nor do I have a grand idea about how to close the gap, I know one person that can help. With The CX Dictionary, Ben has created a single point of reference from which any current or aspiring CX professional can start and, if ever lost, return.

It may seem obvious to say, but we need to know what the terms and references we use in CX really mean.

Having these terms defined and benchmarked is something that will bring an enormous amount of legitimacy to a discipline that suffers from "premature evaluation" and will guide and enrich the broader CX community.

I am proud that I can help to make this happen, and contrary to my initial suspicions, The CX Dictionary is one of the most un-boring books you'll ever read.

James Dodkins
The Customer Experience Rockstar
www.jamesdodkins.com

INTRODUCTION

"What exactly <u>IS</u> Customer Experience...?"

... is probably the most common question asked of Customer Experience professionals every day. The problem with answering this question isn't that there is no definition but is, in fact, the opposite.

Each person involved with Customer Experience can offer an interpretation of what they believe it to be and to mean, and many can debate their definitions very effectively. These interpretations may be narrow or broad, literal or general and are based on the individual's own background, experience and perspective. For example:

"It's a job...It's a mindset..."
"It's consulting...It's a product..."
"It's a department...It's a specialism..."
"It's about talking to people...It's about analysing data..."
"Isn't it all of these things and more..?"

What confuses matters further is that the Customer Experience industry itself has become beset with acronyms and phrases which confuse and confound. Many of those phrases and references point back to older market research conventions. Some refer to the latest technology developments. Others again are general common language terms that have developed specific meanings in relation to Customer Experience practice.

No wonder we've seen an entirely independent language set evolve as the industry surges forward. This can often cause problems when communicating different concepts between clients, agencies and companies, and across sectors, cultures and countries.

"There's no such thing as a stupid question."

This is another phrase we are all familiar with. As the diversity of Customer Experience practice grows, it is easy to feel intimidated by the wealth of information that is surrounding us.

So in an attempt to attack the acronyms, crystallise with clarity and wipe out the waffle, this book will provide the context, background and definitions of CX references for professionals, leaders and researchers working in CX today.

HOW TO USE THIS BOOK

"Really...? But I know how to use a dictionary."

That is very likely true, but this book isn't just a dictionary and is not written in the same formal way. It is also an encyclopaedia, a glossary, a compendium and a discussion of all things CX.

I hope that you will use it as a reference guide and end up reading it like a book, jumping from section to section as you go. (A bit like those fabulous Fighting Fantasy gamebooks from the 1980s, if anyone like me is old enough to remember them).

In particular, if you end up agreeing with some definitions but disagreeing with others, my job is done – because it has got you *thinking*. So go ahead and dog-ear those page corners and cover this book in pencil notes. You have my permission to go crazy.

HOW THE ENTRIES WORK

1. "Customer Experience" will be shortened to "CX" throughout this book, hopefully saving some paper and trees.

2. All definitions in this book are written *in the context of CX.* Sources such as language dictionaries or internet searches may provide more literal definitions. However, the goal of this book is to provide clarity for CX users.

3. You will notice that some entries are listed as acronyms (e.g. CX, PAPI, UX), whilst others are fully worded. This is because I have listed each entry in the form in which it is *most commonly* used.

4. Many words and terms used in CX overlap, so I have grouped similar references under single entries. In some cases, you may be re-directed to a "root" entry elsewhere in the book.

Below shows an example of how the entries appear:

MAIN ENTRY TITLE
Acronyms and alternative names
Main entry text, including:
- Definition
- Examples and use cases
- Advantages
- Disadvantages
- Summary

Also of interest: Links to other relevant entries.

FINALLY...

Thank you for picking up and reading this CX Dictionary. I hope it gives you some helpful insight and clarity in this increasingly complex discipline. Please enjoy the read.

Ben Phillips
December 2020

THE CX
DICTIONARY

A

ACADEMY

The collective initiatives, centralised functions or dedicated departments within organisations which undertake CX training and share best practice.

Companies of all sizes recognise the importance of training staff members and the encouragement of a culture of customer focus. Many have set up their own CX or Customer Service Academies solely dedicated to these activities.

Responsibility for CX Academies can lie with HR or training leaders, who typically roll out specialised training and group classes so colleagues at any level can follow content and attend courses. These may include acceleration of CX knowledge (technically and practically), development of skills to help design better CX journeys and frameworks, and how to better communicate CX objectives and outcomes across organisations.

Many companies issue accreditations for completion of courses so that colleagues can become certified in that companies' own CX initiatives, minimum expectations and unique approach. This level of knowledge can be furthered through individual rank progression and continued personal development for colleagues who may go on to become CX champions within their organisations.

ACCOMPANIED SHOP

A field-based research exercise where a pre-recruited customer will conduct a visit to a specific location and go about a typical shopping experience, whilst observed throughout by a researcher who objectively records details of the customer's visit.

Since accompanied shops are a bridge between observational research (remote) and Mystery Shopping (no observer), the researcher observing the visit should keep their interaction with the customer to an absolute minimum. This will avoid influencing the subject's behaviours and affecting the visit experience itself.

Accompanied shops are used predominantly by retailers who wish to capture precise details of customer in-store experiences at their locations, and therefore will appoint a market agency to provide researchers and to recruit typical customers from panel sources.

Visits may involve full end-to-end experience measurement, including store arrival, navigation and layout, visiting different departments (where applicable), making enquiries, interacting with staff, checking out and departing.

As an extension of Accompanied Shopping exercises, visits to competitor locations are also possible, using the same visit guidance and research criteria, therefore enabling reasonably accurate like-for-like comparisons between brands.

ACTION PLANS

Action Plans are created by departments, teams or individuals to help structure, prioritise and manage CX-related activities using information and outcomes from research programmes.

Many effective Action Planning models exist today, and modern

CX software platforms often include online Action Plan modules that are fed by live survey data.

A well-structured CX Action Plan helps departments, teams and individuals to focus on and unify the effort of improving CX, and should include the following phases:

- Collection of data from a research source such as a customer survey
- Identification of key drivers behind positive CX results and improvement opportunities
- Creation of separate actions to address areas of improvement and also maintain areas of positive engagement
- Identification of costs improvements related to CX initiatives based on physical, time and resource implications
- Prioritization of actions, taking into account relative cost versus predicted benefit
- Agreement on group accountability for delivering change initiatives
- Management of change through regular ongoing milestone reviews and dedicated Project Management
- Reviewing of and evaluation of outcomes
- Repetition of the process (Action Plan initiatives may be cyclical)

Action Planning is a vital component of successful CX programme management where the results of CX programmes are collected for the dual purpose of conducting research and driving positive organisational changes.

Also of interest: CX Platform.

ACXS
Accredited Customer Experience Specialist
The ACXS qualification, provided by the company Rockstar CX, is a global accreditation for practitioners and professionals in the CX industry.

It is a workshop-based qualification which is conducted either in group attendance or individual online format. It follows a modular structure where the taught principles of CX are applied to a hypothetical case study and with relevance to business situations.

Qualifying attendees receive a certificate and the right to use the designation "ACXS" in their formal communications.

AD HOC RESEARCH
Any research work which is conducted infrequently, irregularly or is not continuous, and is likely to require only one round of data collection to arrive at conclusions. The Latin translation of ad hoc means "to this", which in research relates "to this set of results".

There are no fixed methods for ad hoc research and the period is usually a set date range over the short to medium term (a few days to a few weeks). If the research project runs for an extended period, to capture variable results over time, this should instead be considered continuous.

Examples of ad hoc research include:
- A single round of transactional telephone interviews to a target group of customers
- A week of onsite customer interviews at a physical location
- One wave of non-repeatable Mystery Shopping visits

The benefit of conducting ad hoc research is to capture a set amount of workable data and results in a fixed period, which enables close control of the research sample, research objectives and costs.

Ad hoc research is not intended for continuous measurement and is not optimal for capturing feedback results in real-time.

Also of interest: Continuous Research.

ADVOCACY

Advocacy is the act of recommending or strongly supporting a cause, system or belief. In the context of CX, research into customer advocacy helps to define the reasons why an individual will recommend a company, brand, product or service to others.

The term "brand advocate" crosses over into marketing analysis and customer segmentation, where known factors and feedback from customers helps define them as positively-minded towards a brand or product, with a high propensity to repurchase or return.

Advocacy in CX reveals itself in the opinions and feedback of positively-minded customers taken from research and feedback programmes. Analysis of these customers groups can reveal important advocacy drivers, i.e. specific details of why they favour a service, brand or company, and to what level they spread positive word-of-mouth.

Also of interest: Net Promoter Score; Net Promoter System.

ALWAYS-ON SURVEY

Any form of survey which is enabled permanently, rather than sent to subjects using an invitation methodology.

Examples of always-on surveys include links to feedback surveys on website pages, QR Codes situated at convenient trigger points in physical locations, and paper questionnaires which can be deposited in feedback boxes when completed.

An example seen commonly on websites, for example, is a link to a "Feedback" or "Contact Us" page which initiates a web survey when the customer clicks on the link.

Always-on surveys have the advantage of requiring very little maintenance and attract a regular stream of completed surveys from respondents, depending on where they originate.

However, very little intelligence associated with customers who complete always-on surveys can be collected other than through lengthening surveys with further questions. Respondents are "unknown" and, therefore, customer relationship management, loop closure and proactive outreach are far less possible than with known customers.

ANALYSIS
The process of examining data from any source for trends and correlations to provide information and insight. In CX, data sources may include results fieldwork, customer surveys, behaviour monitoring or activity-based information such as purchase data, customer churn, and more.

In CX, analysts review customer data to reveal the drivers behind satisfaction, loyalty, emotional reaction, general impression, brand preference, purchase and repeat purchase decisions and many more.

As a result, many market research agencies and CX software providers have geared their services towards providing insightful reporting through a wide range of analysis methods and capabilities. These can include statistical modelling using established techniques and automated software with features such as AI and Machine Learning.

ANALYST
Any person who conducts research work and reviews and investigates results data for information, meaning and insight.

ANALYTICS
A broad term for the discipline of conducting analyses of various kinds and the production of results of investigative work on research data.

In the case of CX, this data can be collected from research projects or feedback programmes through a wide variety of methods.

API
Application Programme Interface
A set of features and tools which enable direct access between two or more computer systems, operating systems or software packages.

The purpose of an API is to enable an "always-on" link between systems so that those systems can exchange data and information quickly and without restriction.

In CX, API-based systems enable the smoother flow of data between systems which positively impacts the experiences customers have when dealing with service-based companies. An example may be a customer banking system which requires connectivity across various sources to enable a seamless money management experience for the customer.

Many APIs are built by software companies which integrate with client computing systems using standard protocols. A popular API model is known as REST (Representational State Transfer) which enables data exchange and operating capability between web-based computer systems.

ARTIFICIAL INTELLIGENCE
AI; Machine Intelligence
Most commonly known by its acronym, AI is the intelligence of machines and automated systems through taught and learned functions and actions. This is in comparison to natural biological intelligence that is demonstrated by humans and animals.

In CX and research, AI principles have been developed and utilised to assist the processing of large tasks at much faster-than-normal speeds. These include activities such as data sorting, analysis and task duplication.

Examples of AI in practical use in CX today include:

- Automated customer surveying with complex survey routing and branching based on prior question responses
- The use of ChatBots to address inbound customer enquiries without the need for human intervention
- High volume text, speech and social analytics, where large amounts of data taken from text and voice channels are analysed

AI innovations are rapidly advancing in line with the recognition by companies that they need to meet the demands of the customer base both in terms of service fulfilment and relationship management and loyalty.

Also of interest: Machine Learning; Natural Language Processing.

ATTRIBUTE
A specific set of characteristics or features which help to define something, such as different categories of people, objects, services and more.

In CX, attributes are used to describe a set of customer needs or requirements based on customer types and personas, or a series of associations based on research outcomes, such as brand factors. Identifying and understanding attributes enable companies to process data, update and improve services and serve customers in specific ways according to how impactful the attributes are.

Combinations of attributes inform the understanding of what affects variables, and how these will impact research outcomes overall.

Also of interest: Variable.

AUGMENTED REALITY
AR

Most commonly known by its acronym "AR", Augmented Reality involves the blending of artificial, computerised information, objects and imagery with the real environment. Often this takes the form of enhancements of real-world environments by overlaying animated and interactive objects with everyday surroundings.

The principal methods of experiencing AR are currently through devices such as computer screens, mobile device screens and AR glasses or headsets. AR's main applications are in the form of product enhancements and visualisations, iterative design ahead of production, virtual tours, 3-D modelling, audience response and feedback and computer gaming.

The first elements of AR in CX are beginning to be explored with companies now experimenting with AR in training facilities, product interaction and testing, customer interaction and servicing. This can include the transposition of products into real-world environments so that purchasing decisions can be made; for example, clothing, home items such as furniture and even houses (real estate agent virtual tours).

B

B2B
BUSINESS TO BUSINESS
The activities, relationships and engagement between companies, brands or service providers and their business clients.

The focus of CX in B2B is typically on how services between companies impact perceived service and loyalty factors.

B2C
BUSINESS TO CUSTOMER
The activities, relationships and engagement between companies, brands or service providers and their customers.

The focus of CX in B2C is typically on how the impact of services provided or products sold by companies impacts overall customer experience and loyalty factors.

BALANCED SCORECARD
See: Scorecard

BAYESIAN ANALYSIS
A statistical technique which uses probability and prediction to address research questions and objectives. It is named after English mathematician Thomas Bayes (1702-1761).

Bayes's Theorem, published after his death in 1763, proposed that mathematical predictions could be revised based on the inclusion of up to date data. His work suggested that researchers could infer the likelihood of an outcome or a result with a greater degree of accuracy if recent research data or findings update the original base data.

In today's CX research analysis, the principles of Bayesian analysis can be and are often applied, mainly when using inference to show the most likely outcome of a customer research project ahead of commencement or whilst underway. This form of analysis assumes the availability of historical data upon which predictions are based, such as previous results.

BENCHMARKING

In CX, benchmarking is the practice of gathering and comparing research results against similar results from other sources. Data can come from sources such as direct customer surveys, interviews, company performance reports or proactive "scraping" of social media sources.

Benchmarking data reports usually compare companies or countries, or sub-sets such as brands or regions, but is dependent on robust sample sizes to make useful comparisons. The data included must be directly comparable, so the same measurement criteria should be used. For example, Customer Satisfaction scores from surveys using different answer scales would *not* be a useable data set.

A typical method of creating benchmarks is where a research metric generates a score which is used to rank and compare different companies with each other. This enables researchers to produce tables and charts to visualise the broad range of results companies are achieving.

A benchmarking exercise is most effective when it does not only stop with the production of comparable scores but goes on to show where opportunities for improvement exist. The purpose is to ensure that companies identify competitor pull and draw factors and then either improve their products and service levels to compete or, ideally, exceed beyond the capabilities of the competition.

Benchmarking tables are one of the most common reports requested by clients to research agencies working in CX, and enable companies to keep a check on their perceived ranking in the industry.

Also of interest: Norms.

BIAS

Bias in research is the influence of preconceived opinions and perceptions on either the design of a research exercise or a subject's responses to it.

Biased data affects the validity of overall results, so avoidance of bias is an essential consideration in almost all types of survey design to ensure that results are genuine and reliable. It can be introduced in the following ways:

- By researchers, in questionnaires or survey design
- By respondents, in responses to questions and feedback
- By researchers, in reporting and results analysis

Bias may be positive or negative, intentional or unintentional, conscious or unconscious. For example, a respondent answering questions based on a recent experience may answer deliberately negatively to "black mark" the location. This is an example of conscious negative bias.

Meanwhile, a customer with a series of good experiences at the same location may answer the same research questions more positively, even if their most recent experience was average. This is an example of unconscious positive bias.

Techniques to filter out such responses and avoid biased behaviours vary by both the methodology and by the situation.

To prevent design research bias, control techniques include checking of survey design and reporting by secondary teams, emphasis on research codes of conduct (such as ESOMAR and MRS guidelines) and full testing in a pilot phase before fieldwork commences.

To prevent respondent bias, control techniques include close monitoring and pre-selection of appropriate subjects, less reliance on rating scales and fixed responses through the inclusion of commentary boxes, and ensuring the research is not skewed through incentives or rewards for completion.

BRANCHING
Conditioning; Routing
Survey branching, also known as conditioning or routing, is a control mechanism put in place in questionnaire design which directs respondents to different questions based on their previous answers.

Branching can exist in both printed and digital forms. In a PAPI questionnaire, for example, depending on the answer given by a respondent to a question, they may be instructed to answer the next question in the sequence. A different response may require them to miss out the following question and move on to other sections. An example is where males are asked to complete a questionnaire section that is relevant to their gender, whilst females may be asked to answer another. The conditioning question which would control which section the respondent answers would be *"What is your gender?"*

In PAPI, this is a manual process and can be open to mistakes by respondents who complete all questions regardless of branching instructions.

Meanwhile, in digital format, research designers have much greater degrees of control. Dynamic routing controls included in CX software used to build website feedback and mobile app surveys can ensure that respondent answers hide subsequent questions that are not relevant. This ensures greater answer accuracy, a shorter survey completion time and an overall compact and relevant survey experience for respondents.

C

CALL CENTRE
See: Contact Centre

CAPI
Computer-Assisted Personal Interviewing
CAPI is a research method where a researcher interviews a subject using a computer device such as a laptop or tablet to record the respondent's answers.

CAPI remains popular where immediate post-experience feedback and opinion is considered an essential part of a company's research strategy. Examples in CX include where subjects have:
- Exited a store following a purchase or browse
- Disembarked an aeroplane after arrival at an airport
- Departed a restaurant after a meal experience

In all of these cases, the interviewer would be based at a strategic location to approach customers and ask if they have time to answer some research questions based on their experiences.

As per the examples above, the immediate nature of capturing customer responses means that CAPI was a valuable precursor to real-time self-administered surveying in use today. An example of the latter by comparison is personalised email-to-web surveying which does not require an interviewer.

In the cases where self-administered surveys do not provide enough detail, however then CAPI remains a valuable method for face-to-face research situations.

The main drawbacks of CAPI are similar to those of CATI, where the expense of a round of CAPI is typically much higher than a survey programme conducted digitally. Technical issues can interrupt CAPI surveying too, such as failure of the electronic equipment in use for interviews (laptop, tablet, phone screen) and connectivity to Wi-Fi to upload results. In this case, the interview software must be able to store completed interviews offline until an internet connection is established later on, and all interviews are uploaded to a central data collection system.

The confidence of the interviewer to approach customers and accept plenty of rejection before achieving a successful interview is also a drawback in field and CAPI research. Even with plenty of interviewer confidence, the time to accomplish a sample target or quota is also extended compared with fully digital surveys. In this way, interviewers are often located onsite at research locations for long periods.

Also of interest: CATI; Exit Interviews; Field Research; PAPI.

CASE MANAGEMENT
The management of individual customer enquiries, issues or complaints which are known as "cases". These can be raised either personally or on behalf of customers automatically.

Cases form the basis of electronic Closed Loop Case Management systems in which multiple cases from many customers can be dealt with at any time by a team of responsible advisers at varying seniority levels. These are mainly online systems, either standalone (such as a component of a CX Platform) or integrated (into systems such as CRM).

Cases may include customer metadata such as name, account/product type, address and other demographic information, together with details of their enquiry, issue or complaint and a possible survey rating which may have given rise to the creation of the case in the first place (usually a poor service or rating score and a request for contact).

Very often teams handling cases will receive notifications of new cases either through access to a case management system or by emails, and will subsequently attempt to resolve cases within agreed SLA-based time frames and with complete customer satisfaction.

Also of interest: Closed Loop; Service Ticket.

CASE STUDY

An article or piece of original content which shows how successful CX work, programmes, solutions and initiatives have been deployed in any company, industry or country with specific success factors demonstrated. Typically CX case studies are used as sales tools for market research and CX service agencies to show how they have helped and assisted client companies achieve their CX objectives.

A format for a compelling CX case study should adopt at least three key components:
1. The stated business issue(s) and problem(s)
2. The solutions or approaches to overcome the business issue(s)
3. The business benefits of implementing these solutions and evidence of successful outcomes

Clear evidence of successful outcomes may be shown in several ways, including uplifts in tracking CX metrics, increased revenue related directly to CX initiatives, better employee retention, overall more positive Voice of the Customer feedback, etc.

Well written CX case studies should skilfully marry quantitative data (i.e. proof of the successful outcomes) with qualitative information (e.g. cultural and relational improvements and benefits) and tell a compelling and attractive overall story.

CATI
Computer-Assisted Telephone Interviewing
Telephone call interviews conducted between researchers and subjects based on their experiences of companies, products and services. Researchers use a computer software programme to record the subject's answers to questions on the telephone interviews, hence "Computer-Assisted".

Although on the general decline due to the increased popularity of real-time Voice of the Customer surveying, CATI is retained by many research companies to extract rich, qualitative insights from smaller target groups of customers about their experiences.

Using CATI, which can be through cold-calling or booked by prior appointment, researchers can ask longer and more thorough questionnaires about customer opinion, and deep-dive into the specific topics customers feel are important. CATI, therefore, lends itself very well to qualitative research and analysis.

CATI also differs from CAPI since the interview takes place sometime after the experience has happened and does not rely on the interviewer being present on-site to intercept customers.

Due to the longer and less repeatable format of the interview call, CATI is also very well suited to tracking relationship-based factors such as loyalty over time and relationship NPS. Commonly, the CATI questionnaire itself will focus on relationship factors and loyalty drivers, rather than single event-driven aspects.

Whereas automated real-time surveys suffer from not being always able to reach the right respondent, CATI has proved very successful in obtaining feedback from harder to reach customers. These include those in B2B scenarios, or customers whose affairs are managed by third parties, such as private wealth clients. This is because customers in those situations tend to not respond well to general surveys invites via email or SMS, but respond far better to personalised invites and phone-based interview appointments.

CATI does have some drawbacks, such as the process of completing interviews to a sample target being highly manual (e.g. non-attendance at interviews and incorrect phone numbers requiring repeat callbacks). The interview duration and potential questionnaire length also mean total CATI volumes are often low in contrast to other higher volume survey methods such as email-to-web. Furthermore, due to high manual intervention, CATI call programmes are typically expensive. For this reason, CATI is used by companies as a part of a balanced research strategy, and usually only selectively.

CATI is not to be confused with Telemarketing which describes the wholly different purpose of selling goods and services through outbound cold-calling to potential customers.

Also of interest: CAPI; Net Promoter Score; Relationship NPS; Relationship Survey.

CAUSATION
How changes in certain events cause direct changes in other elements of customer experience.

Causation is an underpinning technique in Key Driver Analysis in CX programmes. It is used to identify what factors cause positive or negative changes in outcomes. The relationship between the cause and the effect must be unequivocal, otherwise direct causation cannot be established.

This is different from correlation analysis, which looks at how variables are related to each other both positively and negatively, without necessarily changing them.

An example of causation in CX would be how staff member promotions of specific products lead to increased customer purchases of those items.

Also of interest: Correlation.

CAWI
Computer Assisted Web-Based Interviewing
See: Web Survey

CCXP
Certified Customer Experience Professional
CCXPs are qualified CX professionals who have taken and passed the CXPA's multiple-choice exam paper which covers a broad range of topics.

The qualification requires renewal periodically, and full membership of the CXPA is upheld through ongoing subscription. CCXPs are expected to maintain the best practices and advice of the CXPA whilst they are active members.

A practising CCXP is considered a trusted source of knowledge within a company or at an agency on topics related to CX practice and strategy and can be consulted on a broad range of CX topics by various stakeholders and clients.

Also of interest: CXPA.

CENSUS
An official survey or a count of a large group, typically people, and is therefore related to population-based research.

An example of census-based research includes government-commissioned population counting to determine the number of residents in an area, such as a town or city. Such work is carried out by large market research companies with the resources and field force to be able to cover large geographical areas.

Census research does not explore the rationale or meaning behind data or research results, and is simply the activity of counting and sizing the research sample group, including the categorising and classifying of results within the data set such as age, gender, income and other factors.

CENTRE OF EXCELLENCE
A term generally used in CX to describe a team, a location or a hub of expertise within an organisation where best practice advice and training is provided to ensure high standards of delivery across the workforce.

This typically is oriented around customer-facing service excellence, but can also encompass back office and supporting functions which are not directly customer-facing but do play a significant role in positively impacting customer experience overall.

CHANNEL
The routes by which customers contact and communicate with companies, such as via the web, an app, messaging, social media, phone, in-person or by written mail.

Due to the diversity of these contact options and how customers use and switch between them, many companies understand that effective channel management is essential in helping to provide positive experiences and increase customer loyalty.

CHATBOT
A software program which acts in place of human customer service agents for customer enquiries, enabling short, human-like conversations on a broad range of topics.

Within the past few years, AI concepts have been applied to Webchats, and consequently "ChatBots" have been introduced by some companies to address enquiries and service their customers.

A key benefit of introducing ChatBots in customer services is that they are used to apply the principles of automation to managing large scale tasks. ChatBots do this by addressing common inbound customer enquiries and FAQs where responses to questions are provided through a simple 2-way messaging system. The ChatBot's AI quickly scans the customer's message for common keywords and provides the most likely pre-programmed response, which may include information, advice or further links to other resources. This ultimately reduces the amount of human involvement required for tasks which are relatively simple and highly repetitious.

However, a drawback of the application of ChatBots is that there is a limited range of questions the AI can address, and there is less capability for the handling of complex queries or to continue addressing problems based on existing cases. ChatBots, therefore, service customers using simple "to-and-fro" Q&A whilst human intervention is required to resolve more complex enquiries.

Also of interest: Webchat.

CHECKBOX QUESTION
A format of research question which is commonly used in PAPI, field interviews and in website and mobile feedback surveys.

Checkbox questions are used in CX survey design where multiple answer options should be made available for respondents. This is different from situations where a single answer option, such as in radio button questions or Likert scales, would not fully enable subjects to answer questions accurately or fully.

An example of a checkbox question in use is as follows:

Q: *"Please state which items you purchased in the store today?"*
- ☐ Fresh food
- ☐ Frozen food
- ☐ Clothing
- ☐ Electrical goods
- ☐ None of the above

In the example above, the respondent can select more than one checkbox answer to the question as may be relevant to their experience. Survey designers must ensure that "Not applicable" or "None of the above" answer options are included in questions where alternative answer options are not relevant to a respondent's experience.

A best practice of using check box questions in surveys is to limit the quantity in the same questionnaire to avoid response fatigue and respondent survey drop-out. Because of their versatility, they are a popular method of collecting a large amount of research data in a simple and intuitive format.

Also of interest: Drop-Down Question; Likert Scale; Multiple-Choice Question; Radio Button Question.

CHIEF CUSTOMER OFFICER
CCO
A senior leadership role in the CX industry, many companies appoint a CCO to oversee all customer engagement and experience management.

As a result, CCOs often perform the role of principal stakeholder of both CX and Customer Service initiatives, including CX goal and strategy setting, prioritisation, cost control, service operations and many more functions.

CHIEF EXPERIENCE OFFICER
CXO
An addition to the typical construct of senior leadership roles in modern companies, the Chief Experience Officer (or "CXO" to

avoid confusion with "CEO") leads all CX initiatives within an organisation.

CXOs focus specifically on CX strategy and delivery and generally do not oversee Customer Service Operations – that is the remit of a Chief Customer Officer.

CITIZEN EXPERIENCE
The experience of any individual living within a specific region or country and their interaction with public service departments and government organisations.

Citizen Experience, in place of CX, is used with specific reference to individuals who receive services provided by local authorities and public bodies. These individuals are therefore not customers since, in many interactions with public organisations, no actual purchases of products or payments for services are made.

Citizen Experience strategies and research programmes often focus on and reveal factors which are driven by citizen or user trust, ease of interaction and satisfaction with services. Such programmes do not typically include CX measures such as loyalty, advocacy or recommendation and metrics such as NPS and findings are not compared or contrasted with competitors since in many instances the departments in question are sole service providers.

CLOSED LOOP
Closed Loop Management; Closed Loop System
A system in which customer feedback collected through research surveys is actively utilised to assist the development and improvement of a company's processes, services or products. A piece of feedback from a customer which requires action or follow-up by a company is known as a Closed Loop "case" or "ticket".

Most Closed Loop systems in use today are dedicated software applications such as those found in CX Platforms since the complexity of Closed Loop processes are often too great to be managed effectively using offline systems such as spreadsheets.

A typical Closed Loop workflow would start with research outcomes or feedback from customers fed into a software management system where individuals can determine consequent actions. These are typically pieces of feedback where customers have responded to survey invites with low survey scores, or a particular survey question has triggered a new Closed Loop case.

Depending on the capabilities of the software, users may be able to analyse themes and root cause and addresses issues directly. Customers then receive re-contact (if they have agreed to it), resolution and, if they are satisfied, the case is then closed by the handling agent or employee.

This flow of customer interaction is considered cyclical rather than linear since the process of gathering feedback and reacting to it positively should highlight necessary changes which companies should make to avoid recurrence of similar issues.

Many companies manage Closed Loop processes as a part of their Customer Service strategies, very often through dedicated Contact Centre or online teams, since these agents are on the frontline for customer enquiries and complaints.

There are several factors which determine the design and management of an effective Closed Loop system. These include various "Inner Loop" stages as follows:
- An exact trigger point within research surveys for a new Closed Loop "case" to be opened, with the customers' agreement for re-contact (for example, a low feedback survey score)
- The ability of the service provider to manage case resolution within a short time frame

- The ability of the service provider to manage case resolution with the minimum number of hand-offs between employees

As an extension to the Inner Loop case management stages described above, some companies have adopted the advanced approach of managing "Outer Loops". This is where key learnings taken from the process of customer case management are used to enforce broader company-wide or systemic changes. An example of this may be where continued customer complaints about a company's product influence the redesign of that product for future release.

Examples of outer loop management include:
- The possibility for employees to offer their opinion on the process of issue resolution itself, making suggestions for improvement and highlighting systematic issues
- Integration between a company's Closed Loop case management system and Customer Relationship Management system (CRM), so a full record of resolved cases is retained
- Transparency of overall Closed Loop reporting for business teams so root cause issues are identified and improvements are made; e.g. Complaints team, Web Development team, Product Servicing team, etc.

Closed Loop case management systems are often provided as components of CX Platform and software systems. Using these systems, the case resolution process commonly uses data from transactional surveys rather than relationship surveys due to the immediate requirement to resolve specific customer issues.

CLOUD SOFTWARE
Software which is accessed via various online tools and systems. Data is stored on remote servers and data centres which are not on the client user's own computer network or physical premises.

Through being accessed online, cloud software is therefore very different from On-Premise software which is accessed and hosted locally.

Cloud software in CX offers many advantages such as cost-savings, automatic version updates, increased security controls and accessibility anywhere over the internet. There are no installation and maintenance costs, and licensing fees associated with cloud software services are fixed and regular, allowing for better budget management. Many cloud models also have attractive multi-user rate cards where the volume of users does not necessarily increase overall costs.

Cloud Software differs from SaaS computing in that the term describes a broad system of applications across different networks and systems, all making up the "cloud" in which various services are located. It can encompass a wide array of systems and tools, and multiple components can be used for different purposes, e.g. a remote system for data storage, another for billing and accounting, another for surveying, etc.

Also of interest: On-Premise Software; SaaS.

CLUSTER ANALYSIS
An analysis method where data or research results are grouped or "clustered" together and shown in a visual format such as on a graph. The clusters are formed by grouping together similar results or data points with shared or common attributes.

Its main advantage in CX is to provide a graphical representation of results which are closely related, typically from research which shows satisfaction or loyalty drivers, opinion-based feedback or common themes from customer interviews.

CO-CREATION
The joint participation between a company and its customers, or any other two collaborative groups, to design, iterate and create products and services.

The rising popularity of co-creation as a design principle is due to a growing preference for collaboration between internal colleague teams and external customer groups during product and service design stages to drive successful outcomes.

CX co-creation brings company product and service owners and developers together with engaged Panel and Focus Group audiences to move through various stages of product or service iteration.

The complete life-cycle of a co-creation engagement is initiated through the sharing of a common goal (e.g. design of a new product or improvement to an existing one), through supporting research, onto the analysis of outcomes, sharing of improvement ideas, pilot testing and ongoing modification.

Case studies of successful co-creation principles exist in industries such as automotive, banking, retail, technology and manufacturing.

COACHING

The provision of ongoing training and performance improvement for individuals in a specific area.

Techniques for conducting coaching within companies require two-way interactions between managers or specialist trainers and their staff or subject group members. Coaching differs fundamentally from Training as the interaction in Coaching is usually one-to-one and avoids the use of online modules and certifications.

In CX, coaching can relate to performance measurement and improvement training for individuals managed using CX measures, and the continuous tracking of their performance related to those measures over time.

Many companies prefer that their front-line colleagues working with customers and members of the public as a part of their roles should undertake ongoing coaching and performance improvement throughout their career. This is to stay up to date in areas of service and product knowledge, hone their customer interaction skills and to provide effective brand representation.

Senior-level CX coaching can also be conducted to "upskill" leaders in areas where they may have no prior background.

COMMUNITY
A group of individual members who openly discuss and socialise their thoughts and responses to research topics.

Different to a Research Panel, whose members respond in private to specific research questions and topics, the Community aspect of a Research Community is what sets it apart.

Research Community members become so by responding to invites or adverts from recruiting agencies or community managers and are included in an online forum where research topics are openly discussed and debated. Community members contribute their thoughts and opinions on the topics presented, and responses are monitored and used in analysis and reporting by community research managers.

Community research is becoming increasingly popular with companies who wish to maintain a live and "always-on" research presence, utilising the format to test out respondent reactions and current trending opinion flexibly and dynamically compared with formally structured and less agile Research Panels.

Also of interest: Panel.

COMPLETE
A shortened form of the fuller phrase "Completed surveys", this is used to describe any quantity of surveys which have been

fully completed and submitted for analysis by respondents.

COMPLIANCE AUDIT
Store Audit; Store Compliance
Location-based visits conducted by paid professional auditors used to measure and collect data on the physical and operational status of a location, such as a company high street store or branch.

Often misused and confused with the measurement of CX in physical locations, such as through Mystery Shopping, Compliance Audits should entirely avoid the inclusion of CX data and focus only on the hard facts and information about each location. A Compliance Audit would typically capture data on the following:

- The physical condition of a location
- Whether management teams are following general operating standards and guidelines
- General hygiene standards and maintenance of facilities
- Compliance with Health & Safety regulations
- Availability of stock
- Staff resourcing levels
- Correct display of POS and marketing materials
- Correct display of Public Insurance Liability and Licensing certification

Auditors tend to be career professionals who regularly visit locations to conduct audits, and will announce themselves upon arrival with appropriate ID and will share the findings of their report with location management teams during a post-visit debrief. This is so that management staff can make immediate changes to ensure they are operating the location within company guidelines. Open dialogue with the auditor should also enable the location management team to raise awareness about any ongoing issues which are beyond their control.

Since Compliance Audits should capture only functional and operational information about locations, they should be used in balance with Voice of the Customer programmes to provide a complete picture of location-based performance. This is often not the case, however, and hybrid versions of Compliance Audits and Mystery Shopping are used by some companies in the place of more appropriate CX initiatives, which consequently achieve only part of either goal.

An example of better synchronicity between Compliance Audits and CX would be where a company's VoC programme reveals the key drivers behind customer satisfaction, which in turn should drive the measurement of what impacts those factors within Audit visits. A simple example is where a VoC survey may reveal consistent issues with a retail store's changing facilities, which in turn should be a compliance check for an auditor during a visit.

Due to the very functional nature of Compliance Audits, the overall visit schedules and outcomes are not always overseen by CX professionals and are often run and managed by operational stakeholders.

Also of interest: Mystery Shopping.

COMPLIANCE MYSTERY SHOPPING
See: Compliance Audit

CONSULTANCY
The provision of expert advice in a specific field of knowledge or practice.

In CX, many consultancies established over recent years sell consulting services to help their clients design, measure, manage and improve CX research and programmes. Many of these consultancies are staffed by ex-agency and ex-client CX professionals who have set up practices on their own to advise and guide clients in industry sectors they are familiar with.

CONSUMER

Often misused interchangeably with the word "customer", a consumer is an individual who interacts with a product once or frequently and repeatedly, which is used up altogether, such as through dispensing or eating; literally, it is "consumed".

Since the word "customer" is used to describe a person who has purchased a product or service and has experienced this through one or several touchpoints, the term "consumer" cannot, therefore, be used interchangeably.

Use of the term consumer is most appropriate when referring to manufactured items that can be purchased, such as food, drink, household items, equipment, or any item which has a single or limited usage or lifespan before repeat purchase is required.

Also of interest: Customer.

CONTACT CENTRE
Call Centre

A Contact Centre is any company team, department, division, office or building that is responsible for direct contact with customers based on both inbound enquiries and outbound communication.

In today's highly customer-focused marketplace, Contact Centres are a vital channel for companies to address both enquiries and resolve issues with their customers. The description "Contact Centre" has replaced the term "Call Centre" over time as customer engagement channels have shifted away from phone calls exclusively to include telephone, SMS, websites, email, social media and chat.

Contact Centres are especially crucial for brands who do not own or run physical outlets and branches, therefore are vital for supporting customers either pre or post-sales and for any general enquiries.

Colleagues working in Contact Centres are commonly known as "Agents". Today's virtual working capabilities means that not all agents are based physically in the same office. If full remote-working is enabled for home-based agents, then an agile workforce can support all typical customer interactions. These can be through secure access to online information and customer management systems from different locations and time zones.

Contact Centre operational structures can be complex, with many connected systems and back-office applications supporting agent activity. The success of these systems being able to support agent servicing through phone, web and chat channels has a critical impact on CX and overall brand reputation. For this reason, over time, the Contact Centre industry has become heavily monitored and performance managed, where several standard KPIs are enforced and closely tracked due to their association with general customer satisfaction.

Contact Centres are a specific channel of customer engagement for CX and outcomes seen from research in the supported lines of communication (phone, web, chat) can often be quite different to those seen from face-to-face customer service.

Also of interest: First-Time Resolution; On-Time Resolution.

CONTINUOUS RESEARCH
Any research conducted on any aspect of CX which does not adopt a single project format so continues over time without a fixed end date.

Continuous research takes the opposite approach to ad hoc research which can be spontaneous, is conducted once and is reactive. Continuous research is instead planned, takes place frequently and is very often proactive since measurement can be adapted based on insight gained from previous research rounds.

The term is generic and does not describe a fixed schedule, so patterns of continuous research may include the following examples:
- Daily feedback surveys
- Weekly field research
- Monthly exit interviews
- A fixed range of research in a repeating pattern, e.g. retail store Mystery Shopping

CX professionals and researchers can use continuous research in real-time Voice of the Customer programmes in balance with less frequent, more strategic ad hoc research to support mutual findings or deep-dive on themes which surface from one or other approach.

Also of interest: Ad Hoc Research.

CORRELATION
A form of analysis which establishes a direct link, cause or effect between more than one set of data. In the majority of correlation analysis work, this is between two separate data sets.

Correlation analysis is one of the most commonly used forms of statistical analysis in CX work, especially when measuring a key CX metric. The principle of correlation in CX, therefore, applies to an understanding of what causes better or worse customer experiences, and how data can show this empirically.

A simple example would be to explore whether colleagues recommending add-on items to customers in stores positively impacts increased basket size and higher value transactions. Examination of two data sets might be as follows:
- Customer feedback from research surveys that they were upsold to in a friendly and positive way by store colleagues

- Retail data showing increased basket value and total checkout receipts for the same customers
- In this case, which shows the former positively influences the latter, we can say there is a positive correlation between upselling and customer spending behaviours

A negative correlation (or no correlation at all) would show the opposite.

Also of interest: Causation.

CRM
See: Customer Relationship Management

CROWDSOURCING
Crowdsourcing is the practice of involving groups of individuals to come together to achieve a particular goal, using the resulting "crowd" as the resource to achieve the desired outcome.

In CX, the principles of Crowdsourcing have enabled CX researchers to replace more structured and formal research Panels with more agile and widespread crowds for research tasks.

The benefits of Crowdsourcing in CX include the agile open-ended nature of recruitment online, and individuals are attracted to the relevant research crowd through open invite, advertisement or recommendations from other individuals. Instead of a restricted number of participating researchers typically available in a traditional research panel, crowds used for the same purpose change, evolve and grow based on recruitment needs.

Research conducted using crowds can vary in range from polls, to survey questionnaires to field research and more. Because crowds are more open-ended and agile, CX researchers must understand that the degree of control over responses and the individuals in the crowd themselves is less than with traditional research panel.

It is entirely possible to achieve full results based on sample requirements and targets from a recruited crowd in a matter of hours and even minutes, depending on the complexity of the research task. For this reason, it is common practice that individuals in the crowd who complete research tasks receive some form of small reward or incentive. This in itself is significantly more cost-effective for CX researchers managing the costs of a programme compared to the typical costs of Panel management.

CULTURAL VARIANCE

Natural differences in human interpretation which impacts customer experience, due to the different countries of residence, spoken languages and native cultures of customers.

Examples of cultural variance can often be seen when multi-country research programmes are run, and responses from different countries and cultures can be compared. Some of these differences include:

- Expectations of service levels (what represents both good and bad)
- Interpretations of company branding, communications and marketing
- Preferences for different service models
- How respondents interpret research questions (based on the quality of translations, slang used, etc.)
- How respondents answer research questions with numbered rating scales (use of high 9s and 10s can be rare in some countries)
- Avoidance of full disclosure of opinions (in some cultures, this is perceived as "too" honest)
- The technology used to conduct research (for example, if the research is online, the lack of reliable internet access in some geographies should be taken into account)

Researchers must consider many of these cultural variances when reporting findings. A useful way to compare like-for-like outcomes is to incorporate benchmarking comparisons to identify local or regional anomalies, consistencies and inconsistencies, and trends.

Also of interest: Benchmarking; Multi-Country Study; Tetraphobia.

CUSTOMER
Any individual who purchases products or services from a company or service provider and receives experiences across one or more transactions or touchpoints.

Customers, their loyalty and their opinions are the primary focus for all CX work. As a result, they are the most commonly interviewed and surveyed population in modern research programmes.

Also of interest: Consumer.

CUSTOMER-CENTRICITY
An aspirational status whereby organisations and individuals are driven solely by their customer's needs and requirements, and are utterly responsive to those needs, resulting in total dedication to, dependency on and mutual admiration with their customers.

There is no agreed or fixed rating or scale for customer-centricity and, as a result, there is no single measure by which companies are judged as having reached such a status. Some market research companies have set up their own benchmarking reports and indices, using a combination of different factors, in an attempt to quantify customer-centricity. However, the phrase remains in use moreover to describe the aspirational goal of *becoming* customer-centric.

Consequently, some companies are said to be "more customer-centric" than others, which essentially means they demonstrate qualities associated with a highly customer-focused business, such as:

- Empathy
- Politeness
- Responsiveness
- Proactivity
- Willingness to make right
- Communicating clearly
- Recognition of loyalty
- Listening to customer feedback
- Co-creating
- Saying thank you

The loyalty of many customers to specific global brands is markedly more positive in the instances where those brands demonstrate the qualities above and execute customer service and support on this basis.

For this reason, customer-centricity remains a commonly stated strategic goal among organisations who recognise the connection and correlation between loyal customers and improved profitability.

CUSTOMER CHURN
The number of customers who stop making purchases from or stop using a company's products or services, often expressed as a rate or as a percentage of customers overall.

The reasons for customer churn vary widely among companies. They may include defection to a competitor for reasons due to poor service, faulty products, low brand reputation or that the customer no longer requires the product or service. Attempting to understand the drivers behind these reasons determines the amount of research commissioned by companies in this area.

In CX, calculating or showing customer churn rates is often done alongside results which show satisfaction or loyalty scores such as NPS. Where correlation analysis is conducted, low satisfaction or NPS scores generally correlate strongly with high customer churn, and so it is usually accepted that improved satisfaction and NPS scores will correlate with low customer churn.

Correlation analysis alone does not explain the reasons why customers choose to stop buying from brands, so further research is required to understand these reasons. This often conducted through customer feedback surveys, social media analysis and interviews with customers who are closing accounts or cancelling purchases and subscriptions.

Understanding customer churn is a way for companies to address lost revenue opportunities and enhance brand reputation. It also helps to identify focus areas for potential recovery, provided churn drivers are identified and addressed affirmatively.

Also of interest: Correlation; Net Promoter Score.

CUSTOMER ENGAGEMENT
CE
Any form of direct contact between a company, brand or service provider with customers through selling, servicing, advertising, marketing and proactive outreach.

Customer engagement can take place between companies and their customers in person or virtually, and over different communication channels such as face-to-face, email, telephone, online events, through written literature and social media as examples.

Customer engagement is frequently used within CX as a term to describe the nature of the relationships a company has with its customers. Positive, proactive and transparent engagement is considered a vital component in ensuring long-term loyalty and therefore is a vital component of operating strategies and customer service models.

CUSTOMER EXPERIENCE
CX
The very topic of this book. A simple and deliberately high-level statement regarding CX might be:

"Customers can experience brands, products and services in any way, at any time and anywhere, and the CX profession is built around continually measuring, understanding, reacting to and improving those experiences."

Used as a noun, CX describes not only the practice of researching, collecting, analysing and acting on customer information following product, service or brand experiences but also the profession itself. To say "I work in Customer Experience" means that "I am associated with the industry and its inherent practices". CX professionals typically, therefore, vary widely in their background, and CX roles vary hugely from company to company.

Since a definition like the above is so over-arching, it accounts for why the CX industry of today spans a multitude of disciplines, practices and professional roles. There are both advantages and disadvantages to this situation.

The advantages are that CX is now at almost frenzy-levels of importance at the top levels of companies, and senior leaders are appointed into positions to oversee complete execution of effective and transformative CX strategies and initiatives. This focus and attention mean that CX is becoming embedded culturally, whilst responsibility for delivering positive CX transformation spans many company departments and business verticals.

The disadvantages include the opposite effect from the above. The industry has reached a saturation point where thousands of agencies, vendors, software companies and service providers all claim to have transformational CX approaches and philosophies. In reality, many of these organisations offer point solutions or client services which are neither purpose-built nor scalable.

Confusion can also felt by people seeking to enter the CX industry and by companies seeking to identify and hire experienced CX professionals. For this reason, standardisation of expertise within the CX industry has become essential, just as in other specialist industries that require individuals to have a combination of theoretical and hands-on experience.

Recently, some training and accreditation organisations have attempted to reduce this problem through the introduction of widely adopted and standardised qualifications.

By its very nature, the definition of the term "Customer Experience" and a widely accepted agreement of it remains fractured due to the associated range of practices, disciplines, products and people.

CUSTOMER EXPERIENCE MANAGEMENT
CEM; CXM
The practice of managing CX strategies, activities, initiatives, research, results and improvement.

CXM, as it is known, is an extremely broad description for the various tasks CX professionals undertake within their organisations. Usage of the term is wide and varied, and it does not describe one particular method, solution or approach.

The ultimate goal of CXM is to ensure CX measurement and results provide value for a business; helping to transform service through improvement, enhance brand reputation and maintain customer loyalty.

CXM can also describe other things, and is used variously by different companies depending on the context:
- The process of managing CX research results and reporting

- Loop-closure processes for resolving customer service issues
- The design and implementation of improved customer journeys based on mapping exercises and touchpoint analysis
- Customer servicing across omni-channels
- Software designed to survey customers and manage insight gained through analysis

CXM forms part of overall CX strategy and a structured management approach to CX can help companies to achieve the following goals:
- Identify the unique drivers that impact experience and isolate these for improvement
- Anticipate and predict customer needs
- React quickly to customer demands and changing sentiment
- Redesign and re-map customer journeys based on changing trends and behaviours
- Conduct ROI analysis and linkage of CX to financial performance
- Manage costs effectively and create savings through improved efficiencies
- Increase loyalty and brand reputation whilst minimizing customer churn

Also of interest: Customer Experience; CX Platform.

CUSTOMER EXPERIENCE MANAGER

An individual working in a dedicated CX role who is responsible for day-to-day measurement, management, delivery, reporting, knowledge-sharing and maintenance of existing CX programmes.

A CX Manager may also be responsible for vendor and supplier relationships and contract management, quality control of data measurement and collection and possibly responsibility for a dedicated CX department within their company.

The CX Manager role is the most common CX role within

companies worldwide today and, depending on the size and diversity of the enterprise, there may be more than one CX Manager working within the same organisation. They may have distinct areas of responsibility, background skills, specialisms and business unit alignment.

Experienced CX Managers with CVs that evidence a relevant and robust background are highly sought after in the marketplace today, especially if they are qualified with recognised industry certifications.

CUSTOMER EXPERIENCE MARKETING

The process of targeting marketing campaigns to customers as a result of leveraging information from CX measurement, analysis and insights.

CX marketing heavily borrows from the successes of traditional CX and attempts to meet and exceed customer expectations in terms of outward campaign messaging and personalisation. This is most commonly seen online and through social network advertisements, which are specifically tailored towards the end-user, and focus on the individual's general preferences and predicted needs rather than straight selling such as is done through pure sales marketing.

CX marketing activity may utilise CX insights from research programmes to make specific targeted offers intended to appeal to particular customers.

CUSTOMER EXPERIENCE PROFESSIONAL

An individual working exclusively in the CX industry; whether as an independent agent, consultant or adviser; whether employed by a market research or CX software firm; whether employed directly by a brand or company.

A CX professional's main activities and responsibilities are determined by their employer or industry sector industry, and can therefore be widely varied and unique.

The distinction of "professional" can be validated through background training, individual experience and industry qualifications, although these are not mandatory.

CUSTOMER EXPERIENCE RESEARCHER

An individual working in the CX industry who may be designing, planning, conducting, managing or reporting on CX research programmes and outcomes.

Many variations on this role exist, including CX researchers who are company headquarters-based, working on behalf of a brand or company, and researchers who are employed by agencies, and maybe field-based or working remotely.

The role of CX researcher can be validated through background training, individual experience and industry qualifications, although these are not mandatory.

CUSTOMER INSIGHT

See: Insight

CUSTOMER JOURNEY

The collected experiences of customers across various interactions or touchpoints with companies, brands or service providers.

Customer Journey analysis is a critical component in modern CX, where an understanding of the many interactions customers have with companies over any period helps providers to identify improvements to overall customer experiences. This helps to identify gaps in the experience delivery systems that may already be set up and is an effort towards continual improvement.

Measurement of customer journeys is dependent on the channels through which customers are served. Using the example of a multi-channel business or service provider, this might include the measurement of:

- Physical journeys, e.g. in-store experiences
- Online journeys, e.g. browsing and shopping from a website
- Contact Centre journeys, e.g. one or multiple calls to one or more telephone lines
- Non-contact journeys, e.g. brand reputation analysis or marketing and advertising impact

Journeys themselves may be short, single-contact events or much longer, multi-point events, across more than one of the above channels, and are again linked to the nature of the services and products a company provides.

For example, a customer journey involving the purchase of a cup of coffee from a coffee store, which may only require a single, short engagement, is a very different journey to that of a customer looking to make a far more complicated mortgage application through their bank.

For this reason, a vital understanding of the various touchpoints of different customer journeys and the impact these have on overall experience can be gained through conducting Customer Journey Mapping workshops.

Also of interest: Journey Mapping.

CUSTOMER JOURNEY MAPPING
CJM
See: Journey Mapping

CUSTOMER LIFECYCLE
The period which an individual is and remains a customer of a brand or a company. Understanding, measuring and tracking customer lifecycles is a critical component of CX research and management work, especially in industries where more than one contact or engagement with the same customers are commonplace.

Some customer lifecycles are very short, while others are extended. Therefore analysis and understanding of lifecycles are typically valuable to brands and companies who have continuous customer relationships, such as through the provision of an ongoing service (e.g. an insurance policy) or a supported product (e.g. a computer with a warranty or maintenance contract).

Also of interest: Customer Lifetime Value.

CUSTOMER LIFETIME VALUE
CLV
A calculation or the outcome of analysis which shows the relative financial value of a customer to a company or brand over the period they remain an active customer.

Estimating the financial value of customers has recently become a high profile method of correlating revenues and profitability with CX since the objective of researchers and analysts is to understand the differences between spend levels of customers at various levels of satisfaction, loyalty and engagement.

In most cases, the obvious correlation applies, which is that more delighted, loyal and engaged customers tend to spend more and return to and recommend companies, brands and products more frequently. The opposite is also most often true. Using data which reveals these drivers, companies can focus on what drives satisfaction and what drives profitability to streamline their CX efforts and initiatives and grow their customer base.

There is no one agreed method to calculate CLV, as the factors to establish this will vary between companies, industries and customer types, and the methods to conduct analysis are also diverse. A simple method is to correlate the levels of customer satisfaction from a feedback survey together with the value of some recent purchases. In this example, a hypothesis may be that higher levels of satisfaction correlate positively with higher average transaction values. This research may be made more robust by correlating satisfaction with purchases made over time through multiple transactions, not just one.

Research in this area can become very granular so that detailed examinations of specific drivers behind CLV are made clear, and in this way can become a compelling way for companies to communicate the positive value of good customer experience to their employees.

CUSTOMER PANEL
See: Panel

CUSTOMER RELATIONSHIP MANAGEMENT
CRM
The methods by which a company manages the relationships it has with its customers.

The acronym "CRM" has become synonymous with the software and data systems which enable companies to maintain and manage customer contact and records. Therefore these systems have become integral in the principles of ongoing effective CRM.

CRM systems are large data "warehouses" of customer interaction information which can comprise customer account details, their transaction histories, service types, contact numbers, email addresses, social media activity, marketing preferences and more.

CRM systems are seen as central repositories of essential information and are often integrated with multiple other company systems to enable effective information exchange.

Customer data, housed in data "warehouses" or "data lakes" is accessed through means of the CRM interface, which pulls relevant data records upon enquiry. Examples of such uses include:

- For customer sales and servicing by frontline colleagues
- For proactive marketing by marketing departments and teams
- For historic and ongoing analysis by CX researchers

CRM systems help to centralise customer data from across multiple potential touchpoints. In theory, a fully operational CRM would enable a colleague to view information about a customer from across their telephone, website, location, email, written, video, chat, social media and marketing touchpoints.

Examples of customer data accessed frequently by CRM software users include:
- Accounts
- Policies
- Order & return records
- Full transactional history
- Complaints (and resolutions) records
- Contracts and renewal dates
- Membership information

Many organisations evolve their own CRM systems using programs developed in-house or through leveraging open source systems to create cloud-based data lakes. Others utilise 3rd party pre-built systems; market leaders at the time of writing are Salesforce, SAP, Oracle, Adobe and Microsoft.

Also of interest: Data Lake.

CUSTOMER SATISFACTION
C-Sat; Cust-Sat; O-Sat; Satisfaction
Customer Satisfaction can describe several things depending on the context:
- A general term for customer research
- A name for customer research and feedback programmes
- The outcomes of a specific satisfaction question within a research or survey questionnaire

Broadly, Customer Satisfaction, or "C-Sat" as it is widely known, is used as a catch-all term for all CX work, programmes and strategies within an organisation. Many company CX programmes are therefore known as the "Customer Satisfaction" programme by name, and the term is used to describe any work that sits within the remit of colleagues who have responsibility for customer service and management.

Customer Satisfaction as a specific measure is derived from the outcomes of a single research question based on a format similar to the following:

"How satisfied are you with [brand/product/service] following your experience?"

This varies widely across global use cases in terms of the wording, context, format, scale and application. The question is used to capture not only brand satisfaction but also satisfaction regarding services, people, products, location and many more besides. There is no "one rule" for how the question can and should be used most effectively.

Whilst the wording and context of the satisfaction question itself are widely varied, so also are the answer options made available to respondents, including:
- Simple "Yes" "No" answer format
- Numbered scales from 1-3, 1-5, 1-7 etc.
- Worded response selections on various scales between "Highly unsatisfied" to "Highly satisfied"
- Emojis, star ratings and other visual methods used to encourage high response volumes
- Open-ended verbatim

It is because of the wide variety of satisfaction question design in research that it is generally considered unsuitable for benchmarking and cross-industry comparisons. This lack of comparative ability led to Bain & Co. together with Fred Reichheld, developing the Net Promoter Score question and framework in the late 1990s, where a single consistently worded and scaled question could enable more accurate cross-industry comparisons.

Many users of satisfaction research worldwide have also reported that, although early-stage results show interesting and actionable outcomes, mature programmes often show a satisfaction score "flatline". This can offer very little differentiation in results and insight between data points over time, such as month by month. This lack of variation can present a risk that satisfaction data loses importance and relevance over time and invested stakeholders deprioritize their focus on results as themes become repetitious and static.

Satisfaction measurement remains popular in CX research given its commonality, applicability across all channels, general stability, ease of understanding by respondents, and the ability organisations have to customise the measurement to their requirements.

CUSTOMER SERVICE
The provision of services to people at any point before, during or after a purchase. These services might include advice, guidance, suggestions, information, demonstration, provision of options, order picking, sales process, product support, issue handling, enquiry management and many more elements of service dependent on the nature of the engagement between a brand and its customers.

Front-line Customer Service employees are considered vital in the provision of good customer experience – as they are often the only representatives of brands customers will come into contact when making purchases.

CXPA
Founded in 2011, the Customer Experience Professionals Association is a non-profit organisation offering thought leadership, networking and training in CX activities. The CXPA

aims to bring together otherwise disparate CX practice and advice into a single source of information and to grow its established membership base of CX professionals.

The organisation arranges industry networking events and meetings, publishes articles on CX best practice and sponsors events and conferences worldwide. It also facilitates CX career development through its membership networking and peer events.

As a result of its evolution and growth, the CXPA introduced a CX qualification, known as the CCXP (Certified Customer Experience Professional), which candidates can attempt in a multiple-choice question exam. This can be preceded by optional in-person or online training workshops delivered by accredited trainers which prepare candidates for the exam itself.

Currently, the CXPA counts almost 4,000 members among its growing global membership body.

CX PLATFORM
Software and technology used to create, distribute, monitor, manage, analyse and report on customer feedback.

CX Platforms are essential and extremely popular tools in modern CX management. Many software companies have developed sophisticated platform systems which enable clients to manage the end-to-end process of CX surveying and reporting. Some of the main features of CX Platforms include the following:
- Omni-channel survey creation, formatting and testing
- Company hierarchy management
- Survey distribution and campaign management
- Response capture in real-time or near-real-time
- Triggered alerts based on the latest results
- Customer Closed Loop using Case Management
- Analysis such as charting, correlation and sentiment

- Dashboard-based results reporting
- Push reporting to target users
- Import of external data sources for overlay analysis
- Connection to external systems through APIs
- Integration with company CRM systems and synthesised data from other external sources
- Knowledge Libraries and best-practice information resources
- Customisable features

The first CX Platforms emerged in the early 2000s, developed and launched by tech startups and Silicon Valley-backed agencies. These were initially positioned as automated solutions for projects at smaller scales compared with the large-market research studies executed by the most prominent market research firms.

Momentum soon gathered pace as the tech companies began to win market share, based on their ability to expedite and automate the process of surveying customers and capturing their feedback across multiple contact channels.

Today, many of the original CX Platform companies have since merged with others or have been acquired, and the technology has evolved rapidly to include advanced AI capabilities, innovative reporting solutions and adaptability for different client companies of all sizes and industries. The primary focus of CX Platform companies is now to promote their ability to help clients manage the complete lifecycle of customer experience, not just to collect and help clients manage survey data.

Approximately every 18 months, market research company Forrester release their "Wave" report which reviews the updated position of a select ten leading CX Platform and technology companies, based on their strategy and market presence. Other similar publications are available in the marketplace to help buyers choose between the different technologies.

CX Platforms are used within organisations to provide centralised online resources for multiple users with different roles to access customer feedback information that is relevant to their business areas. Data can be viewed at different levels, including company overall, geographic region or country, brand or service, engagement channel and product. Additional filters can be set to enable these data levels to be viewed by business division or unit, department, location, team or even individual. Even further reporting filters can allow the review of data over various time frames such as day, week, month, quarter, and year.

Dashboards built into CX Platforms are the primary interface users have with the system. They can show metrics and survey scores at an aggregated level (such as NPS and C-Sat), in real-time (as real at data connections will permit) with a range of smaller widgets such as graphs, charts, trendlines and Word Clouds.

The main capability which separates CX Platforms from standard surveying tools is the inclusion of Closed Loop case management, where customer requests for contact following experiences (often to raise issues or to complain) are fulfilled through a ticketing and management system.

Also of interest: Closed Loop; Customer Experience; Dashboard.

D

DASHBOARD
A component of a CX Platform (usually the landing screen) or a stand-alone report which headlines CX scores and key data.

Basic level Dashboards were for some years produced in rudimentary software applications such as spreadsheets, showing research results scores at an overall level and using simple graphs and charts. The highly manual production of these data views led to the development of dedicated software which can achieve more visually attractive and more interactive reporting capabilities.

Modern advanced Dashboards featured in CX Platforms are highly visual and interactive, and can include the following features and functions:
- Score "dials" and graphics showing research results and scores
- Graphs and charts including line graphs, column graphs and pie charts showing results trends and breakdowns
- Word and sentiment clouds
- Customisation features such as move, edit, add and remove reports
- Role or team-specific results
- Single-Sign-On capability
- Data imported from outside sources, enabling correlation and comparison analysis

- Ability to create and save views and favourite reports
- Full admin control of user access and licence distribution

Dashboards are optimised for computer screen usage, although some software providers have created mobile device versions of the same, with limited views and capabilities suited to smaller screens.

CX Dashboards can be provided through SaaS or On-Premise software solutions and have become one of the most popular tools for researchers to visualise CX programme results today.

Also of interest: CX Platform; On-Premise; SaaS.

DATABASE
A collection of information which is organised and stored electronically for access by various users.

Database structures, inclusions and use cases vary widely. They provide an effective way of storing and organising large quantities of information which would otherwise be impractical and difficult to access and use (for example, using paper document filing).

Database information is organised into a series of sheets with rows and columns, and users access information by writing queries in Database Management Systems (DBMS) and access results through user interface screens. These systems may involve familiar "front end" screens based on the popular Windows format, for example.

Many companies have IT systems which incorporate large databases containing customer information and records, and the maintenance of these is essential for customer engagement activities such as phone contact, emailing, marketing and complaints handling.

DATA CENTRE
DC
A physical location where electronic data is stored on computer systems and servers.

Data centres, or DCs for short, can be on the same premises as companies who use the computer equipment, or can be remote where data is stored off-premises. The DC and all its equipment can also be owned by the user company or rented, in which case server space is made available for client companies to store their data securely. DCs may also be set up in "co-location" format, in which case a DC management company provides rack space, power and security capabilities whilst the client company provides and connects their own equipment and conducts their own maintenance.

A DC may be of any size with any configuration of computer and telecommunications equipment and may store a vast quantity of information based on the needs and nature of the client company.

The physical equipment in a DC is typically a series of computer servers which are configured "rack style" and connected via network cables to desktop machines throughout company premises. In the case of remote data centres, these are connected to client company networks via the internet.

DC service providers can ensure the secure storage of client data and information through a strict series of measures and protocols, both in terms of software encryption and firewalls but also physical security such as guarded locations and biometric entry. In the case of CX, security procedures are particularly important since much of the DC content can include personally identifiable information (PII) about customers, their transactions, activities, addresses, account details and so on.

Where DCs are remote, the service provider can enable options such as dedicated client servers where only that client's data is stored, whilst "partitioning" options may be provided for clients whose data is stored on shared servers.

DATA LAKE
Leveraging the principles of CRM, Data Lakes are large repositories of information on just about any topic, from any source and of any size and content. Data stored in a Lake is typically in a raw format and can be both structured and unstructured.

Many technology companies now offer Data Lake capabilities to clients who will benefit from centralising their data resources, particularly any information related to their customers. Before this was the case, many organisations were faced with building connections between legacy systems which couldn't easily communicate or exchange data, duplicated information, were specialised, were customised or were merely redundant. In short, the prevalent issue of "Data Silos" could, in theory, be broken down by centralising the data repository a company uses for all of its information into one Lake.

The positive impact of Data Lake principles for CX is that agents servicing customers can access an extensive and relevant range of historical data quickly and seamlessly even though that data may have existed initially across several source systems.

The potential negative consequences of Data Lake storage are that such repositories may immediately be too large to manage and maintain well. In addition, any stored information may simply be forgotten. A third potential negative is the potential security risk of having all customer information stored in only one place.

The various versions of Data Lake solutions available on the marketplace today include those offered by Hadoop, Google, Amazon, Oracle, Microsoft and many others.

DELIGHT

In CX, "Delight" as a concept refers to the intended positive emotional reaction experienced by only the most highly satisfied customers and advocates. Many companies, therefore, include delight as a goal within CX programmes, using examples of when this is achieved to demonstrate how this successfully improves customer-company relationships.

Measurement of delight is a purely qualitative exercise, typically using verbatim analysis from research and survey results to provide examples and consequently association with service and satisfaction drivers. There is no standard "Delight scale" or consistent form of measurement as with other CX metrics.

For these reasons, delight is considered by some research professionals to be too vague and too open to interpretation to be used quantitatively. Since there is no quantitative element to capturing or measuring whether a customer is delighted, there is no certainty that those same customers will display other key loyalty factors. These might include spreading positive word of mouth, returning, re-purchasing, and increasing average spend.

Therefore the usage of delight in terms of CX research and management is most common not as a hard measure but instead as an aspirational goal at the top level of customer strategies and programmes.

DEMOGRAPHIC

The research of human populations and the data created as a result of demographic studies. This may include different categories of information about individuals, including gender, age, location, income, marital status, etc.

In CX research, demographic analysis is used to create different customer category types, through which service and product experiences are designed differently to meet the needs of those customer groups.

Demographic analysis has therefore been used for many years by companies who service different customers in very different ways and has been a mainstay for market research companies providing those demographic research services.

There is no one set methodology by which demographic studies are conducted, and, in the cases where companies have no up to date or reliable system of information about their customers, research can vary between field interviews, online surveys, CATI and more. The only restriction in research methodology is usually the cost, given the expensive size of customer bases many organisations will possess and will be researched.

Demographic analysis can also be conducted on available company data and information, either resident in a data repository such as a CRM or Data Lake or across multiple systems where customer data is housed. In such cases, no customer interviewing or research is required.

Also of interest: Persona; Segmentation.

DEPENDENT VARIABLE
See: Variable

DETRACTOR
In the context of Net Promoter Score (NPS) research, a popular metric used worldwide in CX research, a Detractor is a respondent who has provided a score of between 0 to 6 in response to an NPS survey.

Also of interest: Net Promoter Score; Passive; Promoter.

DIARY TRACKING
Consumption Diary; Diary Study
A research method in which subjects engage with companies, brands, products or services over a period of time and record their experiences in the form of diary-like entries, with a focus on highly qualitative and emotive feedback rather than

quantitative data alone.

There is no fixed or recommended period over which diary trackers can run, as the focus of the research may vary widely wherever this methodology is used. Some examples in CX include:

- Tracking the physical effects of a pharmaceutical product
- Recording the experience of buying and owning a new car
- Documenting the application process for a new mortgage

In cases such as the above, research subjects are encouraged to periodically record their thoughts, feelings, emotions and the specific events of interacting with the company, brand, product or service. This can be via electronic submission (for example, online forms and templates) or through maintenance of pen and paper diaries.

Completion is self-administered, although subjects may be prompted to update their tracking diaries by researchers managing the programme. Guidance is typically open-ended and, therefore, results can vary broadly in terms of both quality and volume.

Diary tracking is most useful when highly qualitative, longer-term perspectives on experiences are required and is often counterbalanced with high volume, fast turnaround snapshot surveying such as voice of the customer feedback and polling.

DIGITAL MARKETING
The promotion of products and services online and over the internet using websites, mobile apps and email.

Digital marketing, compared to traditional physical and retail marketing, has become prevalent since the introduction of online services in the early 2000s. It plays an important part in CX based on customer impressions of companies and brands through the marketing messages and campaigns they send and use.

DOUBLE-BARRELLED QUESTION

An occurrence in research questionnaire design where a question is worded so that it asks two or more things, potentially confusing the respondent and diluting the focus of the question.

An example of a double-barrelled research question is:

> *"Was the location you visited <u>fully stocked</u> and <u>adequately staffed</u>?"*

In this example, the respondent may wish to provide different answers about the stock and staff levels, but the question design (and possibly the answer options) does not allow them to do so.

To avoid usage of double-barrelled questions, and ultimately poor research design overall, quality control needs to be exercised when constructing questionnaires. This is a reason why pilot rounds should be conducted to test questionnaire structures before going into the field or live production.

DROP-DOWN QUESTION

A form of online research question where a prescribed list of answer options is made available to respondents after clicking an icon such as a downward arrow or cursor. Respondents then select the most appropriate answer from the dropdown list.

Drop-down question formats are often used in online surveys where respondents pick the most appropriate and relevant answer options from those provided. The benefit of using this format is that many answer options can be listed, but only one is selected.

Respondents click on an answer box which reveals the available options, select the answer they want to provide, which in turn automatically populates the response box.

The format is also an alternative to radio buttons, and is more appropriate where lists of answer selections would be too long for radio button selections.

Drop-down questions should not be used in instances where respondents could select multiple answers. Checkbox format questions better serve that.

Also of interest: Checkbox Question; Multiple-Choice Question; Radio Button Question.

DROP-OUT RATE
The rate at which research subjects leave questionnaires or surveys incomplete.

The number of subjects who drop-out of research questionnaires and surveys is usually an indication of whether the research has been effectively designed in the first place.

The rate of drop-out itself can be calculated very simply using a division of the number of completed responses by the total number of invites sent, seen or opened. This can give a percentage or a number based on how users prefer to report completion rates.

Questionnaires that are too long, boring or irrelevant are the main reasons why subjects drop-out. This causes issues for researchers, who will resultingly have an incomplete sample, miss their target quotas or generally receive poor quality responses.

The methodology of surveys, the channels, the context and the timing all additionally impact drop-out rates. Therefore companies may see different research drop-out and completion rates across the different types of research they are conducting.

Also of interest: Response Fatigue.

E

EASE
CES; Customer Ease Score

A measure or metric in CX research which assesses how easy it is for customers to interact with companies, brands or service providers to achieve intended outcomes.

Confusingly, the acronym CES is the same used for "Customer Effort Score". Therefore the measure is sometimes simply known as "Ease".

The correlation of high ease with high customer satisfaction is strong, and measurement of ease in various forms has become popular in modern CX feedback programmes. Examples of some of the positioning of ease in survey questionnaires are as follows:

"How easy was it for you to complete your purchase today?"

"Was it easy to find information on our website?"

"In what ways did our colleagues help make the application process easy?"

Formats for answer options used with this question are highly flexible, including scales, radio buttons, checkboxes and open-ended verbatim.

Once results are collected, calculation of the Ease metric can be handled in various ways, depending on the needs of the company conducting measurement. These can include Net Score format, Top Box, NPS-like-groupings (on a 10 point scale; 0-6; 7-8; 9-10) and more.

Measurement of ease also correlates positively with measurement of effort, where low customer effort = high ease and high customer effort = low ease. However, the concepts of effort and ease can vary in terms of implication and therefore measurement of ease can be asked as a separate or alternative question. A choice over the two may come down to the intention of the research objective, as follows:

- Research objective 1: to measure how difficult, disconnected, problematic or slow a process of experience is, measure using effort
- Research objective 2: to measure how seamless, smooth, connected, quick and simple a process or experience is, measure using ease

Adoption of ease questions in research is becoming more widespread, as companies find this to be a straightforward and actionable measure. It is relatable for employees, can be used to improve colleague training and knowledge and tracked for ongoing improvement over time.

Also of interest: Effort.

EFFORT
CES; Customer Effort Score
A measure or metric in CX which assesses the level of effort customers make to have their enquiries addressed or issues resolved by service providers and companies. It can also be used to gain perception from customers as to how much effort a company is making to resolve enquires and issues *on their behalf.*

Confusingly, the acronym CES is the same used for "Customer Ease Score". Therefore the measure is sometimes simply known as "Effort".

Examples of how effort questions can be positioned in these ways in questionnaires are as follows:

- As a measure of *customer* effort:

    "How much effort did you have to make to have your issue resolved?"

- As a measure of *company/service provider* effort:

    "Did we make enough effort to resolve your enquiry?"

The variations of effort measurement above will subsequently affect the outcomes of research, results management and reporting. In the instance of measurement of *customer* effort, a high rating is undesirable (I.e. the customer has to make too much effort). Meanwhile, in the case of measurement of *company* effort, a high rating is instead desirable (the company are making lots of effort to resolve issues).

There is no standard format for effort questions and is commonly measured in customer surveys using a linear scale very similar to C-SAT (1-5, 1-7, 1-10 scales are all popular) or even NPS (0-10).

Once results are collected, a calculation of the Effort metric can be handled in various ways, depending on the needs of the company conducting measurement. These can include Net Score format, Top Box, NPS-like-groupings (on a 10 point scale; 0-6; 7-8; 9-10) and more.

Correlation analysis is highly possible where effort is compared to C-SAT, i.e. high customer effort = low satisfaction; high company effort = high satisfaction.

Measurement of effort also correlates positively with measurement of ease, where low customer effort = high ease and high customer effort = low ease. However, the concepts of effort and ease can vary in terms of implication and therefore measurement of ease can be asked as a separate or alternative question. A choice over the two may come down to the intention of the research objective, as follows:

- Research objective 1: to measure how difficult, disconnected, problematic or slow a process of experience is, measure using effort
- Research objective 2: to measure how seamless, smooth, connected, quick and simple a process or experience is, measure using ease

Organisations that have adopted effort or CES as a key measure find this to be a very actionable metric, especially when results are tied back to individual agents, departments, service lines or brands. Improvements can be made at these levels to minimise customer effort and increase the simplicity or seamlessness of service experiences.

Also of interest: Ease.

EMAIL-TO-WEB SURVEY
Email Survey
A survey sent to target subjects via email, containing a link which redirects the recipient to a website survey when clicked.

Email-to-web surveys are one of the most popular methods of engaging wide audiences for high volumes of feedback. They are relatively easy to manage, and email is a familiar and engaging communication method for many customers. They are also affordable, since emails cost relatively little (if anything) to send and responses can be collected using a cost-effective CX Platform with reporting capabilities.

The email will take the form of an invite, sent to subjects with email addresses which are taken directly from company record systems. For the email invitation to be effective, it should adopt the following guidelines:

- Personalised to the subject (Dear Mr Smith; Dear John)
- Contain a clear and obvious subject line (to avoid going directly to a junk folder)
- Refer to a recent and relevant interaction
- Genuinely request feedback from the subject
- Encourage the subject to click through to the website survey

After clicking through from the email invitation, the subject's survey experience is much like a typical web survey experience, and they will complete the survey by answering all questions and clicking a final submission button.

Whilst easy to manage and affordable, email-to-web surveys can suffer from low levels of response rate. In recent years, average response rates from CX research using email-to-web invitations has declined due to over-surveying of customer populations. Rather than naturally respond to an invite and complete the survey, subjects either ignore the email, may miss it entirely or only partially complete the website element of the survey.

One way to minimise this is to ask the first survey question *within* the body of the email, as this engages the subject to begin answering the survey. They provide an answer to the first question by clicking on the embedded answer options, which then redirects them to the remainder of the web survey to be completed online. If respondents choose to drop out as they are transitioned to the web survey, the first question they have answered can still be captured and recorded. For this reason, many email-to-web survey invitations which embed the first question in the invite use a key CX metric such as NPS or C-SAT as the lead question.

Email-to-web surveys are also wholly reliant on the upkeep and maintenance of a reliable CRM or central data system from which subject email addresses can be extracted. Without accurate or active email addresses, many email-to-web survey invitations will end up bouncing back or not reaching the intended subject.

Email-to-web surveys can be sent at a frequency which suits the research approach. For example, transactional surveying programmes use email-to-web surveys to invite customers to feedback following interactions which may occur several times per year. Meanwhile, relationship surveying using email-to-web may be used to reach out to subjects only once or twice per year.

When using a CX Platform purpose-built for sending email-to-web surveys, CX researchers can monitor response results as well as delivery rates, open rates, partial completion rates and final response rates. Redesign of email-to-web surveys may at times be required to avoid consistent low response volumes and high levels of respondent drop-out.

Also of interest: CX Platform; Drop-Out Rate; Web Survey

EMOJI

An emoji is a small pictorial image, typically in the form of round faces of various colours, showing different facial expressions which are used as short-form communication, mainly in online and text messaging.

In a CX context, emojis are a novel way to gather customer feedback at high volume in survey questionnaires and feedback forms. These are variously coloured faces ranging from unhappy to happy, in place of numbered or worded selection scales.

Due to the simple nature of an emoji-based scale and the emotional association made with one of the faces, responses collected from emoji surveys can be high volume and are often useful in capturing a groundswell of opinion quickly.

However, unless accompanied by the ability for respondents to provide commentary behind the reasons for their selection, emoji-based feedback doesn't enable rationale behind responses to be addressed effectively in CX research. They are therefore most effective only as a visual indicator and a fun trigger-point for an immediate emotive reaction to an experience.

EMOTIONAL INTELLIGENCE
EI
The ability for an individual to recognise their own emotions and analyse these in light of direct comparisons and their own comprehension of what these mean.

In 1995 Daniel Goleman published his book "Emotional Intelligence" which raised the profile of this area of research and has remained popular since. This was preceded by prior work in the field, but Goleman's book was a clear watershed for modern thinking about how emotions play a critical part in measuring and understanding human interaction.

Goleman's work and others before and since propose a variety of models for approaching studies that involve analysis of Emotional Intelligence. Some of these models include tests for non-verbal accuracy, facial recognition, reactions, empathy, appraisal and ongoing emotional management.

The applications for Emotional Intelligence in CX is related to how customers have emotional reactions to events, interactions and experiences with companies, brands and service providers, how they recognise and accept their reactions, and how these influence their ongoing loyalty and likelihood to recommend.

EMPLOYEE EXPERIENCE
Colleague Satisfaction; Employee Satisfaction; EX; Voice of the Employee

Seen as a research area and specialism in its own right, or often as a sub-set of CX work, Employee Experience or "EX" typically involves a strategy for gathering employee feedback and opinion on job roles, company environment and company culture.

Where EX or Voice of the Employee research is conducted as a continuous feedback mechanism, this is usually done using the structured surveys, issued through private or open invitation (physical or electronic). These contain a range of tailored questions which employees are encouraged to answer in their own time.

EX research is typically conducted only once or twice per year, is highly private (due to the sensitive nature of some of the feedback given) and for this reason, is commonly run and owned by Human Resources teams as well as leveraging the expertise of in-house CX professionals for data analysis.

EX programmes provide an indicator of the general level of engagement a workforce has with its employer. Outcomes are then used in several ways:
- To help understand general feedback and opinion of a company's culture, management style and specific ways of working
- To provide a clear "Voice of the Employee" for leadership teams to digest and act on
- To lead to constructive, open dialogue between line managers and their teams
- To provide an EX result which may form part of a balanced scorecard of overall company KPIs

EX research is never (and should not be) reported at the one-to-one employee level due to the nature of gathering what may be highly personal and role-sensitive information.

In the instances where software platforms are used to provide EX programme reporting, which is very often the case, data views and reports are provided at the aggregated (e.g. department) level with all employee names made anonymous and personal references removed.

Many users of EX research can correlate outcomes with CX programmes results to uncover a linkage between the two areas. The assumption is that positive EX results and scores will result in better customer experiences, regardless of the channel, industry or type of experience.

This assumption must be treated with caution and proper investigation, as positive correlations may not always be possible. An example would be where an employee's positive experience of their role in handling customer complaints might not directly relate to the customer's experience of having to raise a complaint in the first place. In this particular situation, a positive correlation between employee and customer satisfaction may not be possible.

Many examples do exist, however, of companies that have used EX research programmes to evidence a well-regarded employee culture, where employees feel listened to and cared for by their leadership teams, and are therefore attractive to new employees.

In this way, many companies have become ranked in popular trackers which show the "Top Companies to Work For" across different global markets. These act as a proxy for EX benchmark reports, which are made available by some research agencies, but are far less useful and less well distributed than more readily available CX benchmarks.

ENTERPRISE FEEDBACK MANAGEMENT
EFM
A term used from the early to mid-2000s onwards to describe all CX software platforms and applications used for managing the process of surveying customers, collecting data and analysing responses.

The term EFM was applied to any software which served large enterprises (hence the name) where hundreds or thousands of colleagues, representatives or agents engaged with customers all at the same time. The design of EFM software was therefore intended to enable feedback at a large scale to be both manageable and actionable.

Both the acronym and term have fallen out of common usage in the past few years, mainly because the emphasis has switched from CX Platform technology only being possible on a large scale to instead be deployable at any scale. CX Platforms now enable organisations both large and small to survey customers, manage data and report on outcomes with new features, functions and cost models to suit every level, therefore are not only suitable for large enterprises.

More recently the terms "CFM" (Customer Feedback Management) and "CEM" (Customer Experience Management) have grown in popularity based on product evolution, and a user focus which is on the process of the collection and management of feedback information more than the size of the workforce being measured.

Also of interest: Customer Experience Management; CX Platform; Dashboard.

ESOMAR
European Society for Opinion and Marketing Research
Known by the acronym ESOMAR, The European Society for Opinion and Marketing Research was founded in 1947 and was one of the first organisations to create a professional

membership group together with a code of practice to provide regulation for the Market Research industry. It is a not-for-profit organisation.

Today ESOMAR has approximately 6,000 individual members and 500 corporate member companies across 130 countries. Members are typically from research, data, insights and analytics professions and a large number of practising CX professionals are active ESOMAR members.

ESOMAR describe themselves as a "global voice of the data, research and insights community" and offer various membership subscriptions including a Young ESOMAR Society, full Individual and Corporate membership plans. Members gain access to information libraries, market reports, community discussions and dialogue, ESOMAR events and the right to use the ESOMAR mark and certificate.

ESOMAR has also further developed its Code of Conduct, jointly with ICC (International Chamber of Commerce), which follows three core principles:
1. When collecting personal data from data subjects for research, researchers must be transparent about the information they plan to collect, the purpose for which it will be collected, with whom it might be shared and in what form
2. Researchers must ensure that personal data used in research is thoroughly protected from unauthorised access and not disclosed without the consent of the data subject
3. Researchers must always behave ethically and not do anything that might harm a data subject or damage the reputation of market, opinion and social research

These three guiding principles underpin ESOMAR's professional standards, and all members are expected to abide by them at all times.

Also of interest: MRS.

ETHICAL CONDUCT

The application of the general principles of reasonable behaviour in research, so that the integrity, reputation and data of researching companies, research subjects, methods used and research practices are protected and upheld.

Primarily the principles of ethical conduct apply to research companies carrying out work either for themselves or on behalf of their clients. Teams working on research projects are expected to adopt and adhere to that company's own code of conduct regarding project design, management and execution.

The most well-known and globally recognised codes of conduct are produced by international bodies such as ESOMAR and The MRS, and many organisations utilise these codes of conduct as the basis for their own frameworks.

In general, researchers are expected to observe the following principles when conducting project work:

- Protection of the confidentiality of research subjects
- Protection of the privacy of research data
- Avoidance of conflict of interest, bias and inappropriate or unsuitable research design
- Maintenance of appropriate levels of project quality
- Transparency and objective presentation of research results
- Observance of legal and professional requirements in all research work
- Compliance to and consideration of industry regulations

Many variations on the above principles of ethical conduct exist between research agencies and company research departments. Employees are expected to adhere to these standards, and they will often complete internal training courses which reflect their knowledge an observation of the individual principles relevant to their roles.

Also of interest: ESOMAR; MRS

ETHNOGRAPHY

The study of people and their behaviours in their natural environments, such as their homes and places of work, taking into account their race, culture, habits and social customs. It is a form of field and Social Research.

Ethnographic studies are carried out by researchers using primarily observational techniques. This happens most commonly in a subject's home.

Documentation of subject's responses to research topics and questions is common in Ethnography and may include video or audio recordings which are reviewed and analysed later on.

For these reasons Ethnographic studies are also typically highly qualitative, as they rely on interview-style questions and topic prompts rather than self-completion of survey questions by subjects in a quantitative format.

Seen as a growing and important area in understanding critical aspects of CX, many companies conduct ethnographic studies to provide in-depth, story-based insights which can be balanced alongside higher volume quantitative data.

Also of interest: Observational Research.

EVENT RECALL

The process of humans remembering and recounting events to be used in research project data collection and analysis.

In CX, event recall underpins much of the customer satisfaction and loyalty project work which currently fuels the industry and the metrics which are prevalent within it. Research interviews and feedback surveys are all based on the process of capturing event recall, although there are very few systems put in place to validate the accuracy of human event recall.

Where respondent or subject event recall can be compared to actual events, this may lead to the identification of event bias within a research programme, i.e. the subsequent recollection of events may have been influenced by other factors.

This is an important consideration when tracking behaviour and opinion against a set of specific instructions or event circumstances and can therefore either be gauged as biased or not.

However, in the case of most CX feedback programmes, this is less important as the value of this research lies in the customer's opinion, not the accuracy of their recollection of the events of the experience itself.

Researchers conducting transactional CX programmes seek to avoid event bias and improve event recall among customers by collecting responses as close to the experience as possible with short, targeted questions. Immediately afterwards is considered optimal; some hours or days later can result in a correlation with loss of event recall accuracy.

Relationship surveys depend on the recollection of service and experience factors over a broad period, so although immediate post-event recall accuracy is not as vital for relationship survey work, a degree of reasonable event recall is expected. This can be achieved through well-structured survey questions which enable customers to recall previous events and describe their impression of these.

EXIT INTERVIEW

Conducted onsite at physical locations, Exit Interviews are one of the more traditional forms of market research and remain in practice today.

Exit Interviews are relatively easy to set up and manage, typically involving the positioning of an appointed researcher at a physical location to approach customers for interviews upon their "exit" from that location. In Political research, Exit Interviews conducted outside voting stations during periods of elections are also very common, the results of which are known as "Exit Polls".

Exit Interviewers are usually trained and experienced, the advantage of which is that they will target specific respondent types (if doing so is written into the research brief). They will also execute each interview effectively to capture the maximum amount of information in the shortest amount of time.

Another advantage of the face-to-face format of Exit Interviews is the ability to capture qualitative information alongside quantitative, especially where and if voice recording technologies are used.

Because Exit Interviewing is a manual process, frequently involving researchers remaining at interview locations for long periods, programmes are designed with sample targets in mind. Once that sample target is achieved (i.e. a set number of Exit Interviews) the researcher can leave the site they are working at and begin the process of collating and reporting data and findings.

The methods for collecting data during Exit Interviews have changed over the years, initially relying on simple pen-and-paper (PAPI) with clipboard interviewing. For efficiency, protection of collected data and expediency reasons, Exit Interviewers now more commonly use mobile devices such as tablets and mobile phones and complete respondent interviews by using survey software. This can very often enable interviewers to capture data through survey completion offline, using software installed on the mobile device, ready to upload later on when a full wifi signal is found.

Exit Interviews have reduced in popularity over time due to the more advanced feedback management and social media analysis tools that are now available. However, they are still used in some sectors and in countries where internet penetration remains low and if the client commissioning the research prefers personal interview-style research to be conducted.

EXPERIENCE MANAGEMENT
See: Customer Experience Management

F

FACE-TO-FACE RESEARCH
F2F
Interviewing or surveying that is conducted in-person between researchers and respondents.

F2F research underpins many methodologies such as Field Interviews, Door-to-Door polling, Ethnographic Interviews, Exit Interviews and more. It is the basis for PAPI and is most effective in the instances where achieving a set of complete research interviews against a sample target is the main objective.

F2F is obviously not optimal where high volume short-form web-based, phone-based or non-contact research is required.

Also of interest: Exit Interview; Field Research; PAPI.

FAQ
Frequently Asked Questions
A series or library of common customer questions together with pre-written answers which serves as an always-available information resource. These can be provided by companies and brands of all types to assist in addressing customer enquiries and to provide instant support.

FAQs commonly list the most frequent or typical enquiries

customers make and provide standard answers for those questions. The information provided may include process steps to resolve issues, links to supporting documents or other online resources and websites, email addresses and telephone numbers for further contact and escalation or instructional "How To" videos.

Access to customer FAQ resources is most commonly through website links either from main pages or under Help and Contact sections. These can also be provided as printed materials, such as those found in financial policy documents and contracts.

FEEDBACK

Individual opinion and reaction to recent experiences and events. This can be in the form of solicited feedback, in response to a request such as a survey invitation, or unsolicited feedback, provided through any customer communication channel.

In CX, feedback surveys collect large volumes of customer data about recent transactional events, such as store purchases or brand interactions. Feedback surveys can also collect large volumes of data for non-purchase events, such as location-based visits, brand reputational research and general opinion and polling

Although often used interchangeably with the term "research", feedback focusses on collecting immediate, reactive, emotion-led impression and opinion through event-triggered surveying. Feedback surveys are usually short-form and are self-completed by respondents and are submitted electronically.

Also of interest: Survey.

FIELD RESEARCH

A form of Primary Research, Field Research describes any interviewing, surveying or research conducted in the natural environment of the respondent subject. The literal definition meaning outside of the headquarters or offices of an agency's research centre, therefore in the "field". The execution of Field Research is consequently known as "Fieldwork".

In a CX context, this could mean observing customer behaviour whilst they are interacting with a brand or conducting Exit Interviews (CAPI, PAPI) in front of customers following their experiences for opinion and impression.

Ethnographic Studies are also a popular form of Field Research because of the observational nature and extended cycle time of the research process.

Field research offers an advantage in CX where short, focussed surveys will not provide an appropriate depth of respondent information, therefore can involve longer interview sessions and a greater potential richness of insight.

Total sample volumes of Field Research interviews are usually relatively low, and cost-per-interview is more expensive than full digital survey alternatives and is therefore used selectively by companies as part of an overall CX research strategy.

Also of interest: CAPI; Ethnography; PAPI; Primary Research.

FIELDWORK
The product and result of conducting Field Research which generates outcomes for analysis and reporting.

Also of interest: Field Research.

FIRST CALL RESOLUTION
First-Time Resolution; FTR; One-Time Resolution
Typically used as a KPI in the Contact Centre industry, First Call (also variously "First Time" or "One-Time") Resolution is a measure of whether a company can resolve customer issues or enquiries at the first point of contact.

FTR also relates to the total number of contacts a customer has with a company to resolve an issue or make an enquiry. The number of successful first-time resolutions can be expressed as the FTR percentage, rate or score.

Companies who maintain a high FTR% are generally seen as more successful in CX management due to their ability to avoid extended customer case cycles. In Contact Centres specifically, where FTR is most prevalent, high FTR rates mean call agents can work through a larger volume of inbound enquiries and resolve these with high levels of customers satisfaction during a single shift.

High FTR% therefore also correlates well with positive Customer Satisfaction and NPS scores, and can often make up one of several scorecard KPIs on which agents are performance measured.

FOCUS GROUP
See: Group Interview

FORCED-CHOICE
A form of research questionnaire design where the subject is forced to choose an answer from a deliberately restricted number of answer options, usually without a mid-point or "neutral" option.

This method is employed to avoid respondents selecting only middle or neutral answer options to avoid polar responses. In effect, this forces the respondent to make a decision one way or another by choosing which of the available answer options are more important or relevant.

Examples of forced choices include the following:
- "Yes" or "No" or a 2 point answer option on a scale such as "Agree" and "Disagree"

- Answer scales with an even number of answer options which remove the mid-point (which is often perceived as neutral by respondents)

A drawback of using forced choice in research design is that respondents may not feel any of the available answer options apply, where a mid-point or even "N/A" (not applicable) may have been a more appropriate answer option. During the questionnaire design phase, it is therefore essential to identify whether utilising forced responses might give an inaccurate research outcome due to the forded nature of the question response scale.

FRICTIONLESS EXPERIENCE
A general term and aspirational goal in CX which describes any experience that is seamless, well-executed and ultimately highly satisfying for the recipient.

To achieve frictionless experiences, it is assumed that underlying work has already been completed to remove obstacles and issues which might cause customer experiences to be anything but frictionless.

FRONT LINE
A general term describing company employees who are the first to be in contact with customers, ahead of any other colleagues, before any enquiry or issue escalation. These can be employees working in stores and therefore face-to-face, or in Contact Centres where no face-to-face servicing exists.

Front Line employees and the service they provide to customers are seen as a vital touchpoint in the overall customer journey since they can be responsible for the first and often lasting impression customers gain of interaction with a brand.

In recent years, much training and investment have been provided by companies for front line employees, which has resulted in those brands becoming recognised for and synonymous with outstanding brand service. In this light, front-line service is a clear differentiator for successful CX.

G

GAMIFICATION

Not to be confused with "Gaming" (see the following entry), Gamification is the use of common concepts found in games to turn otherwise repetitive and unattractive non-game tasks into more enjoyable and engaging exercises.

Gamification concepts include points scoring, ranking progression, levelling-up, prize-winning and more. Through the application of these concepts to non-game tasks, adoption and engagement in areas such as the following can be improved:
- Learning and education modules for employees
- Feedback survey completion for customers
- Brand advertising
- Information discovery
- Loyalty programmes and rewards

Gamified concepts such as the above have good adoption and participation rates due to game activities being fulfilling and enjoyable in themselves, but also because of the incentive of a target goal or "winning finish" which encourages repeat play. Examples in use today include:
- Distance rank points earned in driving and navigation apps
- Free food and drink items based on frequent purchases
- Game badges and level-up rewards based on fitness achievements

There are several perceived benefits to gamification in the form of mobile applications or desktop software programs. These can include improved engagement with and adoption of tasks driven by outcomes and objectives, increased satisfaction with the experience of completing tasks and enhanced customer reviews for companies and brands who use gamification concepts commercially.

GAMING

Not to be confused with the term "Gamification", "Gaming" refers to the unwanted and often inappropriate behaviour by employees of companies with CX programmes to work measurement in their favour, i.e. "game the system". The purpose of this behaviour is to improve CX outcomes and measures which have an impact on personal or team performance which may also include financial remuneration and reward.

Behaviours to game results can include doing so on behalf of individuals or teams, affecting the outcomes of any measures used to monitor individuals at those levels.

The scope of what can be gamed depends on the construct of the CX programme or measurement. These can include appealing scores from surveys with defined metrics, challenging the results of Mystery Shopping reports and claiming results should become invalid based on reasons beyond individual control. The general approach is for individuals to seek exceptions, often with claims that the research method or measurement used was not applicable in the first place.

Gaming behaviours can often become habitual and build up over time, rather than one-off or isolated. Therefore careful research programme design is required to ensure employees do not identify loopholes which enable them to contest outcomes.

In addition, CX research stakeholders and programme managers in companies should set clear expectations with employees about the levels of challenge which are appropriate for CX programmes. This is because the insight such research offers to employees should far outweigh any resulting improvements or changes to scores and results.

GDPR

The General Data Protection Regulation was enforced in May 2018 across the member states of the European Union and is a regulation which aims to give control to individuals over their personal data and how it is collected and used by companies.

The regulation addresses data protection, data privacy and data transfer and, under its laws, individuals can request access to copies of their personal data records and for these to be removed at any time. Various companies and countries within the EU have their own versions of GDPR specific to their circumstances, but the general stipulations of the regulation are binding law.

A company which holds and manages individual data is known as a Data Controller and Processor, whilst the individual is known as a Data Subject.

The impact of GDPR on CX in 2018 and since then has been fundamental because many CX research and feedback programmes involve the collection of personal data and management of customer records. As a direct consequence, all research organisations, agencies and groups are bound by GDPR to ensure that no data about any Data Subject is captured or unnecessarily retained beyond the purposes of the research itself, and, as above, should make any records available upon customer request.

The GDPR model has been successfully implemented in international law outside the member states of the EU. Countries and companies around the world have adopted many general principles of the safe and responsible handling of customer data.

GROUP INTERVIEW

A structured and organised qualitative research session involving more than one interviewee and hosted and conducted by a fewer number of interviewers.

Group Interviews are a historically popular way of researching sample groups of customers or users in a controlled environment to provide an efficient way of gathering multiple opinions on a broad range of interview topics in one go. They have been used successfully by companies across many different industry sectors for customer satisfaction research, collaborative product design, marketing feedback and more.

Interview groups are made up of individuals who meet a wide range of criteria, and these criteria depend on the interviewing organisation's research objectives. For example, gender, age, persona type, preferences, buying habits, stage of the customer journey, etc.

There is no fixed number of interviewees in a Group Interview, but larger numbers can be challenging to control and hear from individuals equally whilst smaller numbers do not offer a broad range of feedback or opinion.

The Interviewers or Moderators should follow several principles of effective group interviewing:
- Set out the scope of the interview
- Encourage interactions between group members where required
- Enable evenly distributed feedback among interviewees
- Ensure fair and appropriate conduct within the accepted bounds of research practice
- Debrief the group upon conclusion and thank them for participation

The efficient and dynamic nature of Group Interviewing means this format remains popular, and many worldwide and local market research companies offer Group Interviewing services for clients in any industry vertical.

H

HAPPINESS METER

In some parts of the Middle East and in particular in Dubai in the UAE, Happiness is an official measure and indicator of general citizen wellbeing and is a government mandate. In 2016 the UAE launched a National Programme for Happiness and Wellbeing in Dubai. The measurement of Happiness in various research programmes helps to provide a KPI for the maintenance and insight built around this government policy.

In most customer feedback and research programmes in the region, a measure of Happiness is included in questionnaire and survey design. There is no fixed scale or requirement for this, but the measurement deployed should adopt the principles of fulfilling the three key objectives stated in the government's published "Happiness Formula":

- Employees taking pride in delivering excellent services
- Government entities dedicated to making customers and citizens happy
- Customers themselves actively contributing suggestions to improve services and products and consequently help improve overall happiness

Results are presented in an online Dashboard to which different government and regional organisations have access. A "Happiness Meter" rating is included in the online portal which is used to compare scores across participating companies and organisations.

The overall objective of the accumulated results is to provide a picture of the environmental, social and economic factors of living in the region. This effort to combine and contrast results across an entire city is considered unique and is not replicated anywhere else in the world.

HEARTBEAT

Survey invitation timing, often known as a survey "heartbeat", refers to the period between the sending of a survey invitation to a respondent and the time limit placed on that survey for the recipient to respond.

Use of the term heartbeat therefore typically applies to real-time Voice of the Customer surveying rather than more traditional research methods which do not capture responses through automated technology.

It is considered best practice among designers of real-time VoC research that the valid survey response period is kept short, hence the analogy to the survey having a "heartbeat" which ultimately expires.

There is no hard and fast rule for this, but the principles of accurate survey recall should apply to the time limits set for a survey heartbeat and are generally no longer than 24-48 hours after a transactional event has taken place. It is less likely for a respondent to accurately recall the details of their experience for a period longer than this.

If a respondent attempts to complete a survey after this set period has expired, they should receive an automated message on the screen that they can no longer submit it. It is, therefore, good practice for the company who issued the survey invitation to additionally thank the customer for their attempt to respond.

HELP CENTRE
See: Contact Centre

HIERARCHY
The arrangement of an organisation and the levels within it which make up a company's reporting structure.

Company hierarchy and structural levels are important in many areas of CX management based on how customer research data is firstly measured and then reported and represented. This is especially true of CX Platform software, which will often include online Dashboards which show scores and results from different levels and channels across company hierarchies.

Many companies adopt top-down hierarchies with a senior leadership group or "C-Suite" occupying the top level, followed by directors, departments or channels, then middle management teams, then ground force or customer-facing teams and individuals. Other companies have more complex matrix-like structures with more than one line of reporting, all of which makes the understanding of hierarchical composition critical for researchers to deliver measurement to the correct sample and target groups.

Equally, the reporting of insight is only actionable at a functional and operational level if users are given access to it. Once again, a clear understanding of the business hierarchy and where results fall in terms of individual, branch, team, department, area, region or business unit allocation is therefore critical.

HOSTED SOFTWARE
Software programmes which are owned by client users through purchase or licensing, but are installed and maintained ("hosted") at remote data centres that are not on the same premises as users and are accessed remotely online.

Hosted software solutions differ from SaaS software in that they are owned by the user company rather than rented through pay-as-you-go or fixed-term contract agreements.

Companies use hosted software where they may not have
adequate data centre capabilities to site installed software,
preferring instead to outsource to a data centre facilities
provider.

I

INCENTIVE

A reward, gift or payment intended for the subject of a survey which encourages them to take part in and complete it in full.

In CX these are most commonly seen as a promised reward at point of completion of a feedback survey, such as a discount on goods or services, entry into a prize draw or an immediate free item which can be redeemed on location. The incentive is usually made available only when a respondent has fully completed the research exercise or survey.

This is not the same as agreed or contracted payment for conducting structured research exercises, such as payment made to a panel auditor, professional Mystery Shopper, etc.

Use of incentives in CX research and surveying is contentious and was introduced to encourage more significant volumes of survey completes and responses where some agencies and companies were experiencing low percentage rates. However, use of a completion incentive may arguably influence the research outcome itself, due to a subject's inclination to respond favourably through a sense of obligation to do so based on the available reward.

More recently, non-personal rewards and incentives have been offered by some companies for research completion, for example, charitable giving and donations to various causes, and inclusion in final research report distribution based on relevance and interest.

INDEPENDENT VARIABLE
See: Variable

INNER LOOP
See: Closed Loop

INSIGHT
The intelligence gained from any research.

In CX, insight is an essential requirement for companies running general research or functional experience management programmes to help programme owners understand customer feedback and opinion and make improvements to products and services.

INTERACTIVE VOICE RESPONSE SURVEY
IVR Survey
Used frequently in Contact Centre research programmes, IVR surveys invite customers to respond to feedback questions following a transfer to an automated survey, usually at the end of a call experience. Customers then use their voice to respond to survey questions, and the IVR survey technology utilises voice recognition to record their answers.

The survey invite is presented at the outset of the call where customers can state "Yes" or "No" to taking part (opt-in or opt-out). If customers opt-in, their calls are transferred to a voice-based survey at the end of their call, which is usually automated.

The survey will proceed to ask customers questions, and customers simply reply with their answers. Voice recognition software identifies the responses customers provide, whether simple "Yes" or "No" answers or more complex, longer length sentences.

A key advantage to voice-based IVR surveys is the full automation of the customer interview process, which is comparatively much cheaper than conducting an alternative research method such as CATI. Since the process is fully automated, a large volume of feedback data can be built up over time for use as the basis of CX analysis.

A disadvantage is the high level of opt-out which accompanies this method. Many companies try to mitigate this issue by forcing the survey transfer at the end of the call (i.e. no opt-out option is presented). Alternatives include offering an incentive for customers to take part in the survey or tasking live agents to invite customers to transfer to the survey and leave their feedback on the service they have provided.

Also of interest: Keypad Survey.

INTERCEPT SURVEY
A form of website surveying which utilises specific capabilities to target subjects, rather than providing general blanket survey invites such as a website pop-up survey.

Targeting parameters built into intercept surveying software enables survey designers to select the criteria that trigger invites for customers. These parameters may be based on:
- Whether customers are logged in and known or generally browsing
- The web pages customers are visiting
- Prior website activity, e.g. number or type of web pages customers have already visited
- Information or services customers appear to be seeking and using
- Time customers spend on a page(s)
- Activities already carried out; stage of online tasks completed

The intercept web survey experience itself may also have improved features such as top and bottom banners for website pages, or survey questions which appear inline with website page text rather than on top of, such as with a pop-up survey.

A key advantage of using intercept surveys over pop-up surveys is that the likelihood respondents will react to and complete the survey invitation is increased. This is because the invite may be at a more convenient point during an online experience, is less invasive and does not interrupt immediate website activities.

Also of interest: Web Survey.

INTERVAL SCALE
A scale which is separated by point of equal units.
Measurement using interval scales plots data at points of equal distance. This is most useful when measuring fixed constants which do not vary or change in value, such as mileage distances or seconds and minutes.

As an example in CX research, interval scales may be used to show results based on equally separate points of satisfaction.

An interval scale also does not have any fixed upper or lower values, so can therefore show negative values as well as positive; for example Net Promoter Scores that fall below zero.

INTERVIEW
A form of research where individual subjects are asked questions by interviewers, either in person or remotely, such as by telephone. Responses are then recorded by interviewers on paper or electronically.

Multiple interviews may then be collected together to form the overall sample for a full research project.

Interviews differ from surveys in that they are primarily

conducted face-to-face and interviewers capture respondent answers, whereas surveys are typically self-completed and submitted electronically.

Also of interest: Feedback; Research; Survey.

J

JOURNEY MAPPING
Customer Journey Mapping
The systematic identification, categorisation, labelling and production of documentation which details customer interactions with companies and brands across various stages.

Initially a very manual, qualitative and group-focused research method, Journey Mapping sessions or workshops can be conducted onsite or virtually (using conference call technology) by research agencies or by individual moderators with client colleagues and stakeholders.

These workshops are typically conducted with a specific business objective in mind, for example, to identify the complete end-to-end journey of a banking customer making a new mortgage application. In such instances, the complexity of the journey a customer might experience to achieve the goal of a successful mortgage application is what the Journey Map should capture, detail and document.

Whether conducted in-person in group workshop fashion or online using software mapping tools, journey maps take on the form of linear grids with various points of interest or activity along them. These are often visualised as post-it notes of different colours, where participants in the workshop may have added notes to define a critical point in the customer journey which needs to be added to the map. The map itself is often a large physical space such as a blank wall or large sheet of paper, or can also be a virtual space as found within online mapping tools and software.

These points of activity are placed in the journey sequence in which they occur, from the customer's point of view, and maybe accompanied with further notes which highlight back-office processes, IT systems, operations activities or other factors which are not visible to the customer.

Each note may be linked to other notes, based on their relevance and dependency, and in this way a journey map can become highly interlinked and complex depending on the nature of the journey under scrutiny.

The intention of a successful Journey Mapping exercise is to highlight areas of concern and potential barriers to progression for customers on a given journey, revealing systematic blockages, areas of under-investment, employee concerns and frustrations alongside known customer feedback. Participants are expected to work communally as a representative team to use the fully documented map to make business recommendations that will improve overall customer experience.

Production of actual physical Journey Maps is also a typical output of journey mapping work, which some companies choose to print, share and make available to the broader workforce.

Also of interest: Customer Journey.

K

KAIZEN

Of Sino-Japanese origin, "Kaizen" means (variously) "improvement", "good change" or "change for the better", and became wedded to business terminology following investment in Japanese industry by American companies after the end of WWII.

Since first becoming incorporated into business practice at the Toyota motor company, Kaizen has become popular worldwide and has helped to improve processes across manufacturing supply chains.

The main focus of Kaizen is in removing points of inefficiency in a system, usually a production line or process, and thus eliminating waste as a part of the process. It is therefore closely aligned to Lean principles.

Employees working within a Kaizen-lead production environment are expected and empowered to highlight inefficiencies and issues as they arise, reporting these to a manager, who may at that point recommend the application of Kaizen "Plan, Do, Check and Act" principles to the issue. These are known as "PDCA" principles for short. This is also an example of Point Kaizen management, which attempts to resolve specific and isolated instances of inefficiency intensively and rapidly.

Meanwhile, strategic System Kaizen management attempts to resolve much broader, company-wide issues of inefficiency and is thus more expansive and fundamental.

Kaizen principles have subsequently evolved into other modern systems based on industry and application, including the 5S system of Workplace Organisation, which incorporates the stages of Sort (Seiri), Straighten (Seiton), Scrub (Seiso), Standardise (Seiketsu) and Sustain (Shitsuke).

Apart from Toyota in post-WWII Japan, many other worldwide companies have employed Kaizen principles successfully over the years, including Ford, Lockheed Martin, Nestlé, Great Western Bank and Herman Miller.

KEY DRIVER ANALYSIS
KDA
The process of analysing research data and identifying factors within results which relate to behaviour, typically that of customers. These factors become known as "Key Drivers" and are used as known factors within CX programmes to enable service providers to influence customer experience.

Examples of KDA within CX programme management include the identification of factors which positively and negatively influence customer satisfaction, recommendation, loyalty, repeat purchasing, increased spend, reduced or increased # of complaints, profitability and more. With awareness of which Key Drivers consistently impact factors such as these, companies are therefore able to structure CX services, products and training around them to more positive effect.

Methods to conduct KDA include a variety of statistical techniques including correlation analysis (between two or more sets of data), linear regression analysis and multivariate analysis, each of which is used to identify the relationship between data and the subsequent behaviours customers will demonstrate.

A simple example of KDA in CX might reveal the impact of the consistent failure of a service provider to deliver goods on time, below customer expectations, leading to underlying dissatisfaction and loss of market share. In this case, KDA analysis would statistically examine the relationship between service failures and customer dissatisfaction and whether the former is indeed a driver of the latter.

In this way, KDA performs an important function in CX research and analysis to help quantify just how important service and experience factors are in maintaining customer satisfaction and loyalty.

KEYPAD SURVEY

A survey capability used in phone-based research and feedback which enables respondents to answer phone call survey questions using the buttons on their phone keypad. This is a variation of IVR surveys.

Popular in Contact Centre research programmes, customers making calls into Contact Centres are invited to take part in a phone survey typically at the end of the call experience. If customers opt-in their calls are transferred to a voice-based survey, which is usually automated. The survey will proceed to ask customers questions, and the numbered buttons on the keypad are used to respond. These are often structured as follows:

- 1 = Yes
- 2 = No
- 3 = something else (further options)
- 0-9 = rating scales

The advantage of using keypad surveys within Contact Centre CX programmes is that they are an efficient and scalable method of achieving a volume of service feedback over time. Whilst the push-button responses to each survey question are mostly simplistic and binary ("Yes", "No", etc.) customers may also be invited to leave a short recording of their voice to add further qualitative information alongside quantitative data capture.

A distinct disadvantage of Keypad surveys is the very low survey response rate which accompanies the methodology. This is particularly true where survey transfer opt-in or opt-out is offered at the outset of customer calls, resulting in a very high percentage of customers choosing to opt-out. It is also inadvisable to use Keypad surveys for particular scenarios, for example, a dedicated complaints line.

Also of interest: IVR Survey.

KNOWLEDGE LIBRARY
Knowledge Asset; Knowledge Base; Knowledge Platform
The detailed information made available to agents and employees of a company to help inform and continually educate them on a wide variety of customer topics. Knowledge Libraries also help support agents who are live-servicing customers in-call and during chat and messaging support.

Knowledge Libraries are often software-driven and have recently become integrated into agent desktop environments so that they are readily available to agents when logged into company systems. These are typically in the format of dedicated platforms with their own user interface. These are not fixed to a specific working location and can be accessed via the cloud, which helps to support remote agent working.

Knowledge Libraries may include a wide range of information such as general agent FAQs, product details and features, customer options including price ranges, back-office processes, escalation protocols for customer issues and a range of customer engagement tools such as chat, messaging and callback.

The positive benefits of having Knowledge Libraries available to agents is that complex information can be accessed very quickly on a range of topics and product areas. Consequently, the time a company spends training agents before they are ready to serve customers is reduced. The impact on Customer Experience may, therefore, be very positive since time to address enquiries and issues is brought down through instant agent access to relevant information and advice.

Many software vendors have labelled modern Knowledge Library and Management systems as pure Customer Experience tools. However this labelling should be approached with caution since none of these applications enable actual CX measurement, management or analysis, but instead provide the back office supporting assets agents will find useful to help them serve customers efficiently and effectively.

KPI
Key Performance Indicator
A score, metric or measure which is used to quantify an area of business performance, usually at an overall company level.

KPIs are used as a form of performance measurement within companies to help evaluate success against set measures or targets.

In CX terms, this could be a CX metric or measure, derived from the results of a current survey programme or set of research results, combined with other performance indicators such as revenue, profit, employee satisfaction and more.

KPIs are often featured in combined Scorecards which indicate overall company, business unit, department or team performance against a set of expectations and targets.

Also of interest: Balanced Scorecard; Metric.

L

LIKERT SCALE

Named after psychology researcher Rensis Likert (and pronounced "Lick-ert", not "Lie-kert"), the Likert scale is known to most CX researchers as a horizontal flat line. The line has rating options along its length, commonly seen as numbered or worded scales in research questionnaires and surveys.

The usefulness of the Likert scale in research surveys is that it offers a consistent and straightforward question format that is intuitive for respondents to answer through the selection of one answer option on the scale before moving on to any following questions.

Questions using Likert scales can have answer options that are modelled numerically (e.g. 0-10; the NPS scale is a Likert scale). Others can have worded answer options (e.g. disagree, agree, etc.) and there is no defined or fixed number of answer options particular to Likert scales.

A fundamental principle of Likert scale design compared with other linear scales is that the answer options on the scale should be symmetrical, e.g. an equal number of negative possibilities as positive, such as a 5 point scale (2 negatives, 1 neutral, 2 positives). The purpose of this is to ensure even balance either side of the mid-point.

LIVE CHAT

The provision by a company or organisation of live support using online chat messaging between its agents and its customers. Live Chat is rapidly growing as a principle online support channel for companies serving customers today.

Live chat is offered as a service through an available icon, a link on a web page or in a mobile app. Customers would click on that link or icon to open up a separate chat dialogue window and will receive a notification that agents are available to assist. They will be prompted to state their enquiry and add some account credentials.

The benefits of offering Live Chat by many companies today are for several reasons, not least of which is the efficiency of resolving customer enquiries and issues quickly in a channel the customer has selected.

Live Chat support can often be conducted by Contact Centre agents who multi-task and multi-role between handling customer phone calls, or can be run by teams both onsite and virtually using dedicated Live Chat agents.

Each chat can be resolved with a request for feedback on the experience, either by the agent or automatically. This can be provided through a survey link or an instant rating. Transcribed copies of the chat dialogue can also be provided by email for the customer's records.

LONGITUDINAL STUDY

Research which repeatedly measures subjects or data points to build up an outcome which is measurable over time.

Longitudinal studies are used to research how behaviours, events, changes, seasonality and other factors impact respondent experiences over longer periods. There is no set or agreed time frame to determine that a research study is longitudinal, except that it should repeatedly measure and capture data about the same topic more than once to enable the examination of trending in the post-research analysis. Some longitudinal studies run for many years, and attempt to build up a picture of the impact of changes in opinion and behaviour over that time.

Examples of longitudinal studies include:
- Diary Tracking, involving the completion of experience or consumption diaries by research subjects
- Population studies, where the same respondents are asked for their opinion and feedback at several points over time
- Ethnographic studies, where subjects are researched in their natural environments over time, such as their homes

Due to their extended nature, Longitudinal studies provide results which are considered strategic and can often reveal how both internal and external factors have an impact on broad customer experience. They can also be used to identify the effects of positive change and proactive investment, based on changes made by companies, brands and service providers following analysis of previous rounds of measurement.

Also of interest: Ethnographic Study; Population Study.

LOYALTY
The likelihood of customers to remain customers of companies, brands or service providers in the face of competitive pull is understood through measuring and quantifying their loyalty.

Loyalty is a very broad and sweeping term which can encompass general concepts such as the value, measurement, management and forward actions companies associate with maintaining a steady and consistent customer base.

Very generally, a customer is perceived as being loyal if they make repeated purchases, provide positive word of mouth, recommend a company, brand or service to others and are generally satisfied, all while resisting similar competitor offers and services. More often than not, loyalty is positively correlated with increased profitability and at the overall company level, and much analysis has been done within CX to show this relationship.

Customers can be loyal to multiple brands, not just one, especially in industries and service areas where more than one company or brand has a presence (for example, retail).

Loyalty analysis and outcomes must be carefully handled when reviewing the factors behind why individuals remain to be customers. This is especially true in the instance where only one service provider is available (e.g. a rail company that runs services on a specific route). Another example is where the traditional provider-customer relationship model is not necessarily applicable (e.g. a government department which provides state services).

In these cases, the general best-practice principles of loyalty given above may not even apply, and customers may be entirely dissatisfied with the services and products they receive and use but have no alternatives or competitors from which to choose.

Loyalty can also be used as a term to describe a programme or system whereby customers accrue tangible rewards for remaining "loyal" to that brand. In effect, the more they spend and make repeat purchases, the more they can earn loyalty "points" for doing so, which can later be redeemed for physical goods, treats, discounts and more. This is standard practice in the grocery, retail, quick-service food, energy, entertainment and travel sectors and many providers in these industries have incorporated the concepts of gamification into their Loyalty rewards systems to encourage participation.

Also of interest: ROI.

M

MACHINE LEARNING

The ability for machines, systems or software programmes to improve their performance and efficiency over time based on the experience of repeating various tasks and functions. This is opposed to being directly re-programmed frequently by humans.

For this reason, Machine Learning is a version of Artificial Intelligence, since improvements in performance and efficiency occur within the control of the system and without direct intervention.

Instances of Machine Learning in CX include the processing of large amounts of research data over time. In such cases, the treatment, categorisation and analysis of data can become more accurate, faster and more relevant as the machine or systems "learns" from prior instances of performing the same task. E.g. error rates can be reduced, complexity can be increased, and the data set becomes more attuned to the intended outcomes.

Many CX software applications make use of Machine Learning principles, such as data tagging, text analytics, voice analysis, automated coding, social media scraping and more.

Also of interest: Artificial Intelligence; Natural Language

Processing; Text Analytics.

MANUAL CODING
A practice by which large volumes of unstructured data such as customer feedback comments can be grouped and tagged by human researchers who are reading through and grouping these by eye. The "Coding" element comes from the application of any type of code or tag to these sets of data to make them unique and distinct for reporting purposes.

An example might be the manual analysis of collected verbatim from respondents of a research programme, and the requirement to group these comments into two simple lists – one with "positive" comments and one "negative". Researchers might use tools such as spreadsheets or word processing software to group these comments into columns.

The main benefit of Manual Coding is that almost anyone can do it – the principle being that a researcher of any experience can read through lists of data and simply sort those into one or other groups. This is an inexpensive task and is relatively quick to do, depending of course on the size of the data set and the complexity of required groupings.

Whilst Manual Coding aims to indicate as to how much data sits within defined groups, the arrival of automated technology into the CX marketplace has in many cases exposed many issues and problems with the reliance on human Manual Coding. These can include multiple data sorting errors and inaccuracies due to lack of attention or fatigue, personal interpretation and bias in the sorting process, variation in data sorting accuracy between more than one researcher and a limited ability to sort between anything other than binary factors (e.g. Yes/No, Positive/Negative).

As a result, automated technologies such as Text and Sentiment Analysis software programmes have become popular in the last decade, allowing vast amounts of unstructured data to be sorted with much higher accuracy rates. These technologies use the foundations of AI and Machine Learning to "evolve" as they are applied to unstructured data sets.

Manual Coding can be stepped back after a "tipping point" is reached; i.e. where human attention to sorting and coding data can be replaced by software that has developed and learned to a point where it performs the task more efficiently and accurately. Such software solutions are, however, considerably more expensive than the cost of a Manual Coding exercise which is instead based on the time taken to sort through and categorise a data set.

Another limitation of Manual Coding is the inability for researchers to recognise mixed sentiment or where data might be coded under more than one grouping. Researchers typically group such references under only one category, rather than more than one, which would result in double-counting. An example would be a feedback comment such as the following, which includes instances of positive, neutral and negative sentiment (underlined):

"The service was great, but the food was poor. Altogether I think ABC restaurants provide a reasonable service".

Once again, automated software analysis tools provide a solution to this problem by enabling a comment or piece of data such as the above to be split into segments and grouped accordingly.

Also of interest: Text Analytics.

MARKET RESEARCH
MR
Market Research is a broad term used to describe the activities of surveying and research conducted by agencies on behalf of their clients and companies. Agencies who offer research services are therefore known as or categorised as "Market

Research Agencies" and are grouped alongside each other in industry listings and compete against one another for business.

Many of the research activities defined in this book could be grouped under the category of "Market Research", and the largest agencies offering these services have developed specialist departments and areas of expertise to provide their clients optimal guidance, instruction and service.

METRIC
A specific number, measure or set of aggregated data which provides a single, measurable outcome. In CX, metrics are typically a quantified version of research results, whether scored, weighted, correlated or otherwise.

Typical and common examples of metrics in CX include:
- The number generated using the NPS calculation
- A percentage score calculation, for example through research measuring customer satisfaction ratings
- A score representing Ease (of service, of doing business, etc.)
- A score representing Effort (of finding information, of self-serving, etc.)

The perceived value and importance of including a metric in any CX programme is primarily to provide a measurable number, against which rules, targets and expectations can be set. Many companies feel this better ensures standardisation, and that achievement either above or below a metric target leads to either recognition and reward or performance management and improvement.

Many companies have achieved a great deal of success using measurement based on CX metrics as KPIs and subsequently with linkage to financial outcomes. Others have not fared so well, where internal company culture has been shaped negatively by a constant need to achieve "customer number" targets formed from CX metrics, and a consequent number-gaming culture created by disengaged employees.

For this reason, companies vary their usage of CX metrics, either as visible targets to measure and track performance or instead as data which is "held back" by head office researchers. In the latter instance, the outputs and direction gained from CX metric-based insight are provided to on-the-ground teams in bite-sized, manageable and tactical forms.

It is therefore important to consider the cultural impact and perceived value of including key metrics in any CX strategy at the outset.

Also of interest: KPI; Scorecard.

MOBILE APP SDK
SDK: Self Development Kit
A mobile app SDK is a package of software tools for computer developers who can use the kit to install various software features into a company's mobile app. In the context of mobile applications and CX, this is most likely to be a customer surveying capability.

Surveying through app SDKs demonstrates considerable advantages compared to other mobile surveying methods such as mobile-to-web for several reasons:
- The survey mechanism itself is embedded within the company's app so that branding, logos, fonts and other visual features are in line with marketing requirements
- Control of the trigger points for customer responses are also highly customisable
- Customers are retained in the app to answer survey questions, rather than be redirected elsewhere, thus breaking the experience
- The SDK updates with each new app release version
- Client developers retain control over the SDK itself, rather than a heavy reliance on 3rd party support and costs

Implementing a dedicated mobile app SDK can be an effective

way to enhance the respondent experience and ensure greater control over survey formatting and is becoming increasingly popular in CX research today.

Also of interest: Mobile App Survey.

MOBILE APP SURVEY

A survey which is presented to subjects as they browse and use applications on mobile devices such as phone handsets or tablets. This is distinct from a website survey, which is completed on a website rather than within a dedicated app.

The experience a user has when completing a mobile app survey is very similar to that of completing a website survey, but the technology, build, trigger methodology and timing are all very different.

A mobile app survey is built using a mobile app SDK, which is a dedicated set of tools for implementing a 3rd party capability, such as survey software from a technology vendor, into a native app. Many CX software vendors have therefore created or acquired app SDKs, and these are provided to client developers to embed within native apps.

Because app survey capability is embedded within the app, more mobile-specific functionality and control over survey branding and trigger points are possible. Some of the key benefits include:

- Dedicated versions for different mobile operating systems, including Android and iOS
- Survey pop-ups, boxes and rendering designed specifically for the mobile screen and resolution sizes
- Parameter controls for survey trigger points, such as when customers use specific app functions such as payment and checkout
- Control of client company branding, colourways and logos
- Discreet on-screen survey invitations
- "Always-on" links for feedback made available in-app menus

- Integration with CX platforms so response data can be reviewed in real-time

It is considered best practice to design research for the channel in which it is to be conducted. This is absolutely true of mobile app surveys, which importantly ensure that respondents are not redirected away from apps when reacting to on-screen invitations. The survey questions appear one by one on-screen, respondents complete these, all the while remaining logged into their app sessions. They can then go on and complete their transactions, or postpone completion of the app survey until after they have completed their transactions.

Retaining respondents within an app can result in higher response rates than other methods, such as when a web link is presented which redirects respondents to a website survey when clicked. Whilst this may be a convenient solution for researcher program managers, as standard website surveying software can be deployed in this case, this essentially "breaks" the customer's in-app experience, and can result in high drop-out rates and low volumes of survey completion.

Mobile app surveys continue to rise in popularity as a purpose-built and efficient way of researching mobile app channel usage and CX.

Also of interest: Mobile App SDK.

MODERATOR
A moderator is an appointed researcher who manages the conduct of a group interview, panel interview or focus group session.

Group interviews are typically made up of several research participants, and the role of a moderator in these sessions includes the management of the session flow and timings as well as participant conduct and interaction. More than one moderator may take part in group sessions which are very large, splitting responsibilities between themselves.

A moderator should openly encourage discussions among group participants without biasing feedback or opinion or offering their advice. They should steer the direction of the conversation without influencing it, and recognise and mitigate any issues with group dynamics (e.g. one participant dominating and overriding the opinions of others in the group). They should also record and collate outputs and facilitate any group decisions whilst acting as a neutral observer.

Experienced moderators will have run many group sessions across a wide variety of research areas. Their ability to yield high-quality group research outcomes is, therefore, highly sought after in the research industry.

Also of interest: Group Interview.

MOMENT OF TRUTH
Whilst undoubtedly used many times beforehand in everyday language, the phrase "Moment of Truth" was introduced into CX lore by the Swedish businessman and former Chief Executive of SAS airlines group Jan Gosta Carlzon in 1982.

The phrase, more fully "We have 50,000 moments of truth every day", was used by Carlzon with direct reference to the importance of customer opinion and feedback. As a result of this perspective, an unrelenting focus on customer service would be the bedrock of turning around SAS group's fortunes, which were ailing and in negative profit at the time of Carlzon's quote.

Through a programme of significant CX investment throughout the 1980s, Carlzon was able to turnaround SAS's performance to become highly profitable. These initiatives included flight rescheduling to improve punctuality, empowering staff members to resolve customer issues on the spot, and the introduction of group-wide customer-focussed training in the form of Scandanavian Service School. This training model was so successful it was established internationally and was emulated by British Airways and Japan Airlines.

Carlzon's approach to customer-focused management and decision-making was immortalized in his book "Moments of Truth" published in 1987 from the original Swedish "Tear Down the Pyramids") and is considered one of the most effective models for organisational management.

MRS
Market Research Society
The MRS is an independent organisation offering leadership, training and qualifications in research practice.

The Society has a large body of individual members worldwide and is recognised as a regulator of the research industry through its Market Research Code of Conduct. This Code encourages that research companies maintain the integrity of research through ensuring the methods used to measure, collect and report on data generate insights which are reliable and can be trusted.

The MRS offers a wide number of qualifications in research from certificate level through to Masters level, together with Continuous Professional Development that can help individuals record and develop their experience to further their MRS membership credentials.

Also of interest: ESOMAR.

MULTI-COUNTRY STUDY
A research project where measurement of subjects or activities takes place in more than one country.

Also of interest: Cultural Variance; Tetraphobia.

MULTIPLE-CHOICE QUESTION

A format of question which provides subjects with more than one pre-defined answer option, of which only one answer can be selected.

Multiple-choice questions appear with existing lists of pre-written answers underneath them, which are not hidden as is the case with answer options in drop-down questions. They also differ from checkbox questions, where more than one answer option can be selected.

In a multiple-choice question, respondents select the answer that is most appropriate for them and move on to any remaining questions.

Multiple-choice question formats are used where researchers wish to predefine the answers respondents will consider. An example is as follows:

"How satisfied were you with your visit experience today?"

- Option 1: Very satisfied
- Option 2: Somewhat satisfied
- Option 1: Very unsatisfied

In the example above, respondents can only answer one of the available answer options to complete the question.

Also of interest: Checkbox Question; Multiple-Choice Question; Radio Button Question.

MYSTERY SHOPPER

An individual recruited by a Mystery Shopping agency to conduct a Mystery Shopping visit and complete a full report of their experience.

Also of interest: Mystery Shopping.

MYSTERY SHOPPING

Used predominantly in retail and location-based research, Mystery Shopping involves extended visits or interactions with brands conducted by paid Mystery Shoppers who take on the role of actual customers.

Mystery Shopping as a specific methodology should not be confused with Compliance Audits, which focus instead on the measurement of the physical and operational status of a location with no elements of CX included.

Mystery Shoppers visit various parts of their chosen locations, making observations and engaging with location staff through various scenarios and then return home to create a written report of their visit experiences. These reports are then made available later to location management teams for use in ongoing staff training and overall service improvement initiatives.

The paid nature of these visits enables longer research questionnaires than could be possible in a customer feedback surveys, and reports are often divided up into sections which reflect the natural flow of a customer's visit through a location.

Many companies use a full programme of ongoing Mystery Shopping visits to gather rich CX insights from multiple reports. These visits can often be repeated many times a year to each location by different Mystery Shoppers to provide a diverse spread of experiences.

Many examples exist of where Mystery Shopping is applied to businesses other than retailers, such as in Mystery Calls to Contact Centres and Mystery Dining experiences in bars, restaurants and food & drink outlets.

The Mystery Shoppers themselves are hired by research companies either directly or from a Panel of registered customers. They are provided with a set of guidance notes, including specific scenarios to explore or areas of particular focus during a visit. A minimum standard of performance is expected of Mystery Shoppers as they are being paid by research companies in the format of an extended workforce. Therefore visit activities are closely managed to ensure quality and compliance to visit expectations.

The main advantage behind the "Mystery" element of Mystery Shopping is that it avoids the practical problems and bias caused by announced research visits. Clandestine visits by Mystery Shoppers are therefore seen as a way of measuring more natural, and representative location-based experience as many genuine shoppers might do.

Disadvantages of Mystery Shopping over other research methods include high cost-per-visit, longer set up time and lower volume of final sample in the form of reports. Managing full rounds of Mystery Shopping programmes can also be highly manual, involving shopper management and quality oversight and controls. Additionally, negative internal culture can often build up around Mystery Shopping programmes when these linked to staff performance reward and remuneration, which is ultimately considered poor practice in the research profession.

For this reason, many companies now deploy a small number of Mystery Shopping visits as a "check and balance" against a much higher volume full VoC feedback programme, using the opportunity for rich qualitative feedback from Mystery Shopping reports to embellish insights drawn from VoC surveys.

Also of interest: Compliance Audit.

N

NATURAL LANGUAGE PROCESSING
NLP

The ability for computer systems to understand, organise and analyse different written and spoken human languages. NLP is a form of Machine Learning and is not to be confused with the fundamentally different Neuro-Linguistic Programming (also NLP).

Technologies which utilise the principles of NLP are said to have "NLP engines" which enable the processing of language-based input data at high speed, using both programmed and Artificial Intelligence in some cases.

Examples of NLP that are applied in everyday life include:
- Grammar and spellchecking software built into email or messaging tools
- Voice recognition software built into virtual assistants (e.g. smart speakers, mobile phone assistants and in-car entertainment systems
- ChatBots built into online "Contact Us" chat systems

Many more examples exist and are gathering pace in terms of complexity and application.

NLP is also utilised in CX software applications such as Sentiment Analytics, where various languages are analysed and grouped under different levels of sentiment. Other examples are Speech Analytics and Voice-to-Text transcription, where NLP recognises spoken wording and analyses sound files and converts speech into written text.

Also of interest: Artificial Intelligence; Machine Learning; Text Analytics.

NEAR-REAL TIME FEEDBACK
See: Real-Time Feedback

NET SATISFACTION
A method of calculating an overall net score from a set of customer satisfaction research results. The purpose of doing so is to enable the grouping of responses and subtracting one set from another to provide a single net satisfaction score overall.

See the following entry "Net Score" for an example of how such scores can be calculated.

Also of interest: Customer Satisfaction; Net Score; Top Box Score.

NET SCORE
The method of creating a single overall score from a set of results by grouping data together and subtracting one from another, usually bottom scores from top scores. The consequent number is a net score and is used to simplify outcomes down to one single figure, having taken into account both negative and positive results.

A method for calculating a net score from a range of research results, such as a numbered scale question in a feedback survey, would be as follows:
1. Split the scale into a top grouping and a bottom grouping, depending on the number of data points on the scale scale

a.   E.g. if the research question uses a 1-7 scale, top group = 6 & 7 results and bottom group = 1, 2 & 3 results. Ignore 4 & 5
2. Total the results in each group, i.e. the total of all 6 & 7 responses and total of all 1,2 & 3 responses
3. Create a percentage for each group by dividing each of the 6 & 7 and 1, 2 & 3 totals by the total number of respondents across all results (1-7)
4. Subtract the bottom group from the top group to give a net score

The principles of calculating a net score are to show what a "true" number might look like once low results have been offset against high results. This is a different approach to Top Box score analysis, which only takes into account high scores.

A secondary benefit of net score groupings is the ability to address each of these groups themselves affirmatively, separate to the final net score calculation itself. For example, analysis of all 1, 2, and 3 scale responses from the example given above may enable customer dissatisfaction to be addressed with a more targeted series of remedial actions.

Net score calculations and usage can therefore be found in many CX programmes which track key CX metrics such as satisfaction and Net Promoter Score itself.

Also of interest: Net Promoter Score; Net Satisfaction; Top Box Score.

NET PROMOTER SCORE
NPS
One of the most popular measures used in CX worldwide today is Net Promoter Score or NPS for short, originated by Fred Reichheld and a team of consultants at Bain in the early 2000s. This work resulted in the publication of several books on the subject, including "The Ultimate Question 2.0" in 2006, which was co-authored by Rob Markey.

Measurement of NPS is possible across a wide number of research methods and can be triggered through different customer engagement scenarios. Subjects are presented with a single research question:

"How likely is it that you would recommend this company, product or service to a friend or colleague?"

Variations on this question wording are both possible and permissible as use of the NPS question has expanded across so many industry sectors since its inception. It is important, however, that the general intention of the question wording is retained (i.e. as a measure of the likelihood of recommendation).

It is commonly accepted that NPS can serve to measure CX at two different levels:
- Transactional, or tactical, also known as "tNPS"
- Relational, or strategic, also known as "rNPS"

Of the above, transactional NPS focusses on the measurement of a customer's likelihood to recommend following a very recent single event or transaction. Meanwhile, relational NPS focusses on the customer's likelihood to recommend based on their experiences over time, and consequently possible multiple events and interactions. Research programmes which measure both tNPS and rNPS can therefore show quite different NPS results, even though the measure and calculation method are the same.

Respondents answer the NPS question using an eleven point linear scale from 0 to 10 on which they can only make one answer selection. NPS advisers and users worldwide also strongly recommend this is followed up with a further open-ended question which asks why the respondent provided the answer they did. There is no specific or fixed format for this follow up "Why" question, but importantly should enable the respondent to provide as much commentary as possible regarding their rating and relevant experience.

A calculation is then performed on the responses gained from asking the NPS question, using the following steps:
1. Total the number of responses between 0-6 = Detractors
2. Total the number of responses of 9 and 10 = Promoters
3. Ignore the number of responses of 7 and 8 (Passives)
4. Calculate % scores for both the Detractor and Promoter groups by dividing those subtotals by the total number of responses overall
5. Subtract the Detractor % from the Promoter %
6. The resulting number, expressed as a straight number (_not_ a percentage) is the Net Promoter Score

...i.e. this is the net score of Promoters remaining after Detractors have been subtracted from the overall results. The result will be either a positive number from 0 to 100, where the number of Promoters outweighs the number of Detractors, or a negative number from -1 to -100, where the opposite is true.

Passives are not counted in the NPS calculation since they are considered to neither feel negatively nor positively about an experience and are thus unlikely to either detract or promote based on original NPS research.

The main advantages of using NPS compared with any other metric in CX measurement and research such as C-Sat (Customer Satisfaction) is the consistency of the scale and the calculation. The scale should not be changed (it is always 0-10), the groups of Promoters (9 & 10), Passives (7 & 8) and Detractors (0-6) are fixed, and the net calculation is always performed the same way as above.

As a result, benchmarking has become naturally associated with NPS research. Companies and brands of all sizes can compare NPS like-for-like and based on the number alone. Its simplicity is favoured by many as its greatest advantage, resulting in many advocates of the measure worldwide.

There has also been considerable work done over time to align NPS with overall company financial performance, wherein some companies have shown strong correlations between high NPS, above-average profitability and financial stability such as share values. As a result, many company cultures have evolved around NPS as a critical component of customer-focus, and the metric has been incorporated into performance scorecards at overall, division, department, team and individual levels.

However, many NPS users dislike its blanket approach to measuring customer experience and perceive NPS to have several disadvantages. These include:

- Volatility at low response numbers
- Inapplicability in certain scenarios (e.g. complaint management)
- A propensity for users to substitute the "0" answer option for "N/A" (due to poor questionnaire design)
- Misuse of the scale by respondents to only express extremes at either end of the scale (0 or 10; i.e. polarity)
- That NPS is a measure of likelihood to recommend, not a measure of the certainty of anything
- Cultural acceptance of the question and variations in the translated meaning of "recommend"

Furthermore, some users dislike that a heavy reliance on NPS promotes number-chasing and gaming by company employees, especially where NPS results are built into employee remuneration and reward packages.

Overall, NPS is used today in many ways. These include tracking or serving as an indicator of customer loyalty; to be correlated with satisfaction; in ongoing management of customer groups; as a key component of Key Driver Analysis, particularly through linkage to overall company profitability.

Also of interest: Net Promoter System.

NET PROMOTER SYSTEM

Use of the term "Net Promoter System" is based on a recent adaptation of the principles of Net Promoter Score and the work initially done by Fred Reichheld and Bain & Co. in the early 2000s. Net Promoter System takes the concept beyond that of a tracking number alone (the results of the NPS calculation). It is based on how analysis of these results should have a broad impact across an organisation seeking to leverage its benefits, therefore resulting in a system of processes and changes which become embedded into normal organisational operating rhythm.

The system assumes that NPS has become adopted by an organisation to track its CX performance and that the results of NPS research are used widely and commonly across the organisation's departments to close customer loops and create positive change through improvements to products and services.

Also of interest: Net Promoter Score.

NOMINAL SCALE

A label or an identifier for a group of data, which is used to determine a category, enables nominal scaling. Nominal scaling is used to identify and separate groups of research subjects or any set of research results.

For example, research respondents who live in the North of a country might be grouped under the category of "1" whilst respondents from the South grouped under "2". "1" and "2" in this case are examples of nominal data groups and can be used within nominal scales.

NORM

A baseline or benchmark score, number or data point against which to compare other data. In CX analysis, Norms are used to understand the distribution of research results or scores. This helps to define the range and spread of the results against which single data points can be compared.

An example of the use of Norms in CX research might be to help identify percentile groups in a ranked report, such as the bottom 25% performing company stores in a Mystery Shopping programme.

CX Norms are used alongside CX Benchmark data to help researchers understand the distribution of results when conducting competitive analysis.

Also of interest: Benchmarking.

NPS
See: Net Promoter Score

O

O-SAT
See: Customer Satisfaction

OBSERVATIONAL RESEARCH
Any method which involves researchers watching subjects behaving naturally, interacting with an environment and where results are recorded and analysed, can be considered observational research.

In CX, typical observational research methods include physical customer journey assessments (e.g. store walk-throughs), accompanied shopping trips and elements of ethnography.

OMNI-CHANNEL
Used generically in the market research industry to describe a programme, solution or research strategy which uses all possible customer engagement channels to provide services, enable communication or conduct research surveys. The meaning of the word "omni" stems back to the original Latin for "all".

An example of an omni-channel customer engagement strategy would be one which includes the ability for a company to talk to its customers and vice versa through use of physical (face-to-face), digital (website, app, chat) and voice (contact centre). Customer contact and the ability to switch engagement channels should be seamless, and the customer intelligence that is built up should be based on the integration and exchange of data collected across each of these channels.

Note that the prevalent use of the term omni-channel is often as a catch-all for *any* customer contact, marketing or research strategy when in many of these cases "Multi-Channel" would be a more appropriate term. This is particularly true where only some of the available communication channels are being maximised to manage customer engagement, but not all.

OMNIBUS SURVEY

An Omnibus survey is one which incorporates questions from a wide range of subject areas and is frequently conducted on behalf of more than one client company.

The purpose behind this is to provide companies that have restricted research capabilities, budgets, time and other constraints with access to results from a much broader respondent base than usual.

Client companies participating in Omnibus research will provide their contributions to the survey in the form of focus areas, or specific questions which the research agency managing the Omnibus survey will compile into one questionnaire. To avoid an unnecessarily wide degree of variance in research objectives, the research agency will usually advise clients on these focus areas and provide recommendations for the style and type of questions to be included.

Once the survey work has been conducted and results are compiled, all companies contributing to the Omnibus survey have access to the results, therefore benefitting from the broad scope of the research.

Data collection methods for Omnibus surveying can vary, and the choice will be based on the advice of the agency managing and conducting the survey process. These can include telephone interviews, web surveys and face-to-face interviews.

Omnibus research was (and still is) used by some companies who cannot manage or support CX research programmes directly. However, it is significantly less popular today based on the advancements made in real-time feedback management and the ability to conduct wide-ranging research cheaply and efficiently using online self-service software.

ON-PREMISE
OP

A software application or program that is installed on servers and machines at the owner's or user's premises. This is the opposite of Cloud or SaaS software, which is installed on remote servers and Data Centres.

The advantages of On-Premise software include:
- The close control of the versions that are installed on networked machines
- Management of costs based on how many users are offered licences
- Confidence in data security since information will be stored on local servers
- Offline capabilities, since the software is not reliant on an internet connection
- Adaptability and customisation vs off-the-shelf Cloud or SaaS equivalents

However, the modernisation of accessibility and security features in cloud computing now means that many users of traditional On-Premise software have transitioned their services to Cloud equivalents. This helps companies make further cost savings, increase remote user access and benefit from a broad range of services available in the Cloud.

Also of interest: Cloud Software; Hosted Software; SaaS.

ON-TIME RESOLUTION
OTR
A variation of First-Time Resolution, OTR is a measure of whether customer issues or enquiries are resolved in an acceptable timeframe based on agreed internal standards and customer expectation. It is used typically within Customer Service organisations and Contact Centres who may have implemented several set standards by which they manage customer interactions.

A typical example of OTR is that seen in automated email responses where an organisation may pledge to "resolve enquiries within 48 hours". Many organisations use OTR as a measure of the success of managing more complex issues, where simple FTR would not be applicable (e.g. an enquiry requires multiple transfers, escalation or further investigation).

Timeliness of customer issue and enquiry resolution are known to be key drivers of overall satisfaction within CX research and management. Therefore OTR remains a key KPI within Customer Service and Contact Centre resource planning and performance scorecards.

Also of interest: Closed Loop; First-Call Resolution.

ORDINAL SCALE
A simple method of categorising any set of data or research results in rank order, usually from highest to lowest.

An example of an ordinal scale is the ranking of importance of various service factors for customers in a CX feedback programme. Where "Price" is most important, "Value" is second and "Availability" is third, then the categories "first", "second" and "third" are all examples of ordinal data categorisation.

OUTER LOOP
See: Closed Loop

OUTSOURCING

The extension of business activities, customer services and support from an organisation to a 3rd party company.

The 3rd party company will then provide supporting activities on behalf of the hiring company, acting in their name and as an extended part of the client company's workforce.

Outsourcing is often required by companies who cannot provide resources, staff, premises or services to manage a broad customer base. Outsourcing also offers hiring companies the flexibility to scale up and scale back the required supporting workforces based on changing business conditions and specific project requirements.

Examples of outsourcing can be seen in industries such as Financial Services, Customer Services and Automotive where companies will outsource teams to handle high volumes of inbound customer enquiries.

In Market Research, outsourcing takes the form of agencies subcontracting service providers such as panel providers, technology firms and customer panel to fulfil key research objectives and projects.

Shortfalls in service standards beset the outsourcing industry throughout its boom in the 1980s and 1990s, and some industry sectors became synonymous with poorly delivered service, especially in the case of off-shored customer services.

Today, CX measurement is used as a gauge of how successfully a subcontracted outsourcing company is providing services on behalf of its hiring company and is often the basis on which contracts are initiated, re-negotiated, extended or ended.

P

PANEL

A group of individuals who are members of an organised list of research respondents is collectively known as a "Research Panel". Panel research has been popular for many years as a version of Group Interviewing, which does not necessarily rely on either face-to-face or live assessment or engagement.

Panellists sign up to become members either through invitation or having responded to an advert by the company owning and managing the Panel. Each panellist is then selected to take part in specific research projects based on qualifying criteria such as their age, gender, location, type, etc.

Panels can be built up, managed and used for research in several different ways:
- Provided by Market Research agencies who have constructed dedicated research panels over time
- Created internally from scratch using a self-service panel management tool and through direct recruitment campaigns
- Bought as a single "block" of customer contact details where those customers have already agreed to provide their data for research purposes

Research using Panel can be conducted in any number of different ways, and this is entirely up to the agency or company managing the research process. The most common methods are structured surveys completed online, ad hoc poll questions completed online or by SMS or CATI calls by phone.

Panellists receive a notification that they have been selected to take part in a research project either through a direct invite or call. Any response they provide is private, which is different from how response data is treated in Community Research. All results are then collected by the research team and analysed for forward action and reporting.

Panels can be re-used multiple times, and panellists can be sent numerous research questions for different projects for more than one client or more than one topic. For this reason, many companies maintain active Research Panels alongside their customer measurement programmes for a balanced and rounded view of customer opinion.

Also of interest: Community; Panel Survey.

PANEL SURVEY
A survey which is conducted using respondents who are members of an organised research Panel.

Panel surveys can be of any format and any variety since research requirements will vary widely between agencies conducting the research and their clients, and the usage of a panel of respondents does not determine nor dictate the chosen research format.

Also of interest: Community; Panel Survey.

PAPI
Paper-and-Pen Interview
Known by its acronym PAPI, Paper-and-Pen-Interviewing is research conducted using only traditional paper forms and pen, which are either filled out by a respondent independently or by a field or face-to-face researcher whilst interviewing the respondent.

Before the advent of technologies used for surveying today, PAPI was one of the only ways of gathering large volumes of insight from research subjects. PAPI questionnaires were deployed in situations which made their completion feasible, such as:

- On international plane flights and long train journeys
- During overnight hotel and destination holiday stays
- As patient questionnaires during appointment waiting times

PAPI is mainly used in situations where longer respondent dwell times (and consequently completion times) are possible.

PAPI questionnaires are often long, with multiple questions and many pages making up the form itself. Since respondents can take time to make answer selections and change their responses, PAPI cannot be considered a spontaneous form of feedback.

There are several reasons why PAPI research has declined in popularity in recent years:

- Paper consumption, printing and distribution costs
- They are not designed for quick-fire short form feedback at high volumes
- Mobile and web surveys have become more prevalent, more convenient and are more cost-effective
- They do not permit data capture from a high proportion of the response base
- They do not enable effective feedback management or loop closure
- Collection is very manual and time-consuming
- A high rate of non-completion, where respondents fill in only parts of the forms and leave other sections out, give up or spoil the form through boredom or frustration
- Many forms are lost leading to unnecessary wastage
- Overall response quality and subsequent customer intelligence through analysis can be low

In markets where internet penetration is still catching up, PAPI methodology can sometimes be seen in use, but overall is in decline for the reasons given above.

Also of interest: CAPI; CATI.

PASSIVE

A respondent who has provided a score of either 7 or 8 in response to an NPS survey.

NPS Passive respondents are ignored in the first part NPS calculation (Promoters minus Detractors) but are counted as a part of the overall respondent total.

In NPS results analysis and feedback management, researchers focus on Passive responses as an important source of insight regarding what improvements can be made to both services and products.

Passive respondents can often be the largest percentage of respondents from a set of NPS research results, and therefore changes to this percentage can impact NPS results overall either negatively or positively.

Also of interest: Detractor; Net Promoter Score; Promoter.

PATIENT SATISFACTION

A specific area of research within the healthcare industry, Patient Satisfaction borrows the concepts of general customer satisfaction. It applies these to research work conducted within hospitals, doctor's surgeries, private health facilities and health centres.

Research for Patient Satisfaction generally focusses on areas such as the quality of care, perceived expertise of medical staff, avoidance of appointment waiting times and standard of care facilities, among other key research topics.

Methods for conducting Patient Satisfaction research are widely varied, including personal interviews on-site at medical facilities, feedback surveys following appointments and also diary tracking where the after-care or impact of a prescribed drug or treatment can be tracked.

Also of interest: Customer Satisfaction.

PERPETUAL LICENCE
A software reference which describes the nature of access a user would have for a software tool or resource such as a CX software platform or a computer application.

The perpetual element refers to access being provided for an end-user indefinitely so that access would not expire after a contract period has ended or a single-fee payment (usually in advance) has expired.

Benefits of software packages sold under perpetual licence agreements are that these are often affordable one-time-fee products and a subscription is not required. However, the negatives often outweigh the positives, since perpetual licences do not typically benefit from regular version upgrades and eventually will be shut down and no end-of-life service support offered.

The majority of CX technology, platforms and solutions sold today are provided on a SaaS basis, and require ongoing subscription agreements and include the benefits of regular version updates, maintenance and support.

Also of interest: SaaS.

PERSONA
The grouping of customers with similar characteristics and representation of these customers as a single individual.

Personas of various types are used to create recognisable and relatable identities. They have become popular across many forms of research to show and share customer needs, preferences, behaviours, traits and to predict likely future requirements.

Personas are created by collecting data from existing resources or research and then grouping results under common themes. Analysis of the key factors which make that particular customer group unique from others can then be conducted. The process of doing this is commonly known as Persona Mapping.

Research, sales, marketing and CX management functions have made use of personas for many years to define the key attributes of different groups of customers and consequently design advertising, services and products to suit their needs.

The outcomes of persona research can show fictionalised versions of customers based on the aggregated information that sits behind their "type", accompanied by visuals and data that reflects their attitudes, behaviours, goals, preferences, motivations and more.

Whilst personification of customer types is valuable for the reasons given above, the outputs are mainly qualitative, do not cover all possible customer types and scenarios (leading to marginalisation of "outlying" personas) and do not enable decision-making without further in-depth research taking place.

Persona-based insights and Persona Mapping are highly prevalent in modern CX management. These enable companies to identify core and target customer needs and preferences and design entire CX strategies around these various customer types, resulting in entirely different service models, product design and end-to-end experience delivery.

Also of interest: CX Marketing.

PERSONALLY IDENTIFIABLE INFORMATION
PII

Any information related to a research respondent or general consumer which can be used to identify who they are. This information may include an individual's name, contact telephone number, email address, home address and other data related to who they are and ultimately enable them to be identified. Individuals are known as data subjects under the terminology of GDPR and similar global data protection regulations. (You and I know them as customers).

Under these global data regulations, use of PII data is now heavily restricted. The general principles of the regulations mean that any captured PII data should be deleted and removed from company records and computer systems if that data is _not_ directly relevant to the ongoing management of the relationship with the data subject.

An example of PII data which might be retained is a subject's account transactional histories such as payments. An example of data which would need to be removed is respondent customer feedback and opinion data.

PII data management is closely tied to CX project work, especially in the case of real-time transactional Voice of the Customer programmes. It is, therefore, a significant consideration in the planning of new customer research programmes how identifiable customer data included in the research is retained, redacted or removed. This is to ensure the integrity and value of the research and the customer's right to privacy.

Also of interest: GDPR.

PING-PONG SURVEY

A survey sent via SMS which requires subjects to reply also using SMS, resulting in to-and-fro "ping-pong-style" conversations.

Ping-pong SMS surveys are quick, accessible and easy for subjects to complete, and do not require internet access as with online surveys. Depending on the nature of the questionnaire design, respondents can reply with ratings, numbered answers or full commentary, using their handset keypad.

Ping-pong SMS survey invitations do not immediately redirect subjects to web surveys using an embedded survey link; this is instead known as SMS-to-web surveying.

Ping-pong is especially useful in countries where mobile internet penetration is low and can generate high volumes of immediate, actionable real-time feedback.

The length of each SMS message is restricted to the standard 160 character limit. Therefore researchers designing ping-pong surveys have to ask concise questions to avoid each question running over into two separate SMS messages. It is also considered vital for SMS questionnaires to be limited in length. In other words, the total number of SMS sent in each conversation with respondents should be very few otherwise drop-out rates will increase exponentially.

A drawback of ping-pong surveys is that each SMS sent across a mobile network carries a cost, usually known as a "credit", and multiple SMS back and forth with respondents can quickly increase the overall cost of a ping-pong research programme.

Also of interest: Drop-Out Rate; SMS Survey; SMS-to-Web Survey

POLARITY
An expression in CX research which describes results or findings that are in direct opposition to each other, i.e. at opposite "poles".

An example is where results show only respondent selections from the extreme ends of survey scales (e.g. highly dissatisfied vs highly satisfied), ignoring all other selections in between. Another example would be the grouping of views respondents express during qualitative interviewing into directly opposite clusters, such as only positive or only negative.

Polarising research outcomes is, therefore, a straightforward way of categorising and identifying high-level findings, but is not considered a deep enough investigative method to uncover key drivers behind CX and how research results enable action or resolution.

POLL SURVEY

A form of research which asks single, quick-fire survey questions of a broad and non-targeted audience.

Polls surveys are typically conducted through websites, where a broad audience can have access to and see the research question, which can be on any subject imaginable. Poll respondents can then answer the question through the selection of predefined answers such as in drop-down lists, selection of radio buttons answer options or enter their own verbatim responses. The data is collected and aggregated to give simple, high-volume feedback on the poll topic.

Respondents may also be shown the current results of the poll immediately after they have submitted their answers. These can be seen in the form of an online pie chart or graph, showing a count of the % of responses against each answer option.

The purpose and value of poll questions compared with more structured and lengthier research methods is that they give very quick, snapshot information from a broad audience on a specific topic.

The drawback of this approach is that no fine levels of detail can be achieved, no sampling is made possible, and very often the reasons behind why respondents have answered as they have done cannot be understood or analysed.

POP-UP SURVEY

A form of website survey where a new window or "pop-up" box appears on top of the web page subjects are browsing, which invites them to complete a short online survey.

The survey can either be completed by subjects immediately, postponed until after they have completed activities on that website, or dismissed and rejected.

Pop-up surveys are among the most popular form of website survey and are relatively easy to implement and to manage. Many CX software vendors have built survey design tools that researchers can use to create and deploy pop-up surveys. Usually, all that is required is for new programming code to be written into a web page so that the pop-up invites appear to potential respondents.

Pop-up surveys are completed within the boxes or windows that appear on top of main website pages and can be expanded to full-screen size.

Pop-up surveys are commonly seen and are therefore recognisable to respondents, easy to implement and manage and very affordable at scale. However, they are also an invasive way of seeking feedback as invites interrupt customer browsing experiences and online activities. Consequently, they receive one of the lowest rates of survey completion compared with other research methods, sometimes as low as less than 1% of the number of invites presented.

To ensure maximum participation and the reduction of drop-out rates, pop-up surveys should be as short as possible, with questions that are focused and relevant, otherwise a poorly timed, placed or designed pop-up survey can result in a negative customer experience itself. Some companies offer incentives for survey participation and completion, such as claimable items, loyalty rewards or entry into prize draws.

Also of interest: Web Survey.

POPULATION STUDY
Research which focusses on subjects which are selected from the general population, and are targeted for specific reasons and particular research objectives.

Examples of selection criteria include demographic factors such as age, gender and area of residence, or other factors such as income type, account type, buying preferences and currently loyalty ratings.

Methods used to conduct population research vary widely, and can include everything from individual poll-style questions through to longer questionnaires, and can be completed digitally, by telephone, in person and using self-administered techniques.

Conducting population studies enables CX researchers to pinpoint the opinions and feedback from specific customer groups and to consequently make improvements to services and products most frequently used by those population groups.

Also of interest: Demographic; Longitudinal Study

PREDICTIVE ANALYTICS
The analysis of current and historical data from a variety of sources to identify patterns that can help predict future research results. It is a blanket term for a wide number of statistical methods which may be used to forecast outcomes and results.

In modern analysis practice, the methods and tools for mining the information to be used for predictive analytics have become advanced, and many make use of AI and Machine Learning capabilities in software programmes to make predictions. Very often, predictive analysis methods result in single scores or metrics comprised of more than one factor which are, in turn, used to project eventual outcomes.

In CX, the purpose of using predictive analysis is to build on trended information, past knowledge, known customer behaviour and other measurable information to plan improvements to services, processes, products and general customer engagement.

Analysts can use source data from CX research to plot and predict future results, and examine the impact and cause and effect of changes that may positively or negatively influence ongoing research outcomes.

PRIMARY RESEARCH
A market research reference which involves the collection of new data from research interviews, surveys, and other collection methods to be used in data analysis.

Also of interest: Secondary Research.

PROMOTER
In the context of Net Promoter Score (NPS) research, a popular metric used worldwide in CX research, a Promoter is a respondent who has provided a score of either 9 or 10 in response to an NPS survey.

Also of interest: Detractor; Net Promoter Score; Passive.

PSYCHOGRAPHIC SEGMENTATION
A form of analysis which groups subjects based on psychological characteristics such as their beliefs, preferences, behaviours, opinions, conscious or unconscious responses or emotions.

This is different from traditional Segmentation Analysis, which groups subjects by factors such as location or gender.

Also of interest: Segmentation.

Q

QR CODE
Quick Response Code

A technology which utilises unique codes in the form of complex printed black and white square images which are used to trigger links to online information when scanned using mobile device cameras. The mobile devices require recognition software to be installed to enable QR Code scanning.

The codes contain links to information about company brands, products and services and can be used to advertise items or divert users to interesting and engaging online content. They were first used in Japan in the early 1990s in the motor vehicle manufacturing industry.

CX has since found a practical application for QR Codes, which is that website surveys can be triggered when customers scan QR Codes with their mobile phone cameras. Upon scanning the code, the customer will be redirected to a mobile website survey which they can complete and submit.

This has a considerable advantage compared with other types of survey invitation such as website surveys or email surveys as QR Codes are not sent via any means to target subjects. They are instead made available as a type of "always-on" survey which can be printed and permanently sited at convenient points for customers to scan, such as:

- In-store checkout locations
- Restaurant table talkers
- Shopping Centre information points

The fact that QR Codes are made available for anyone to respond to also presents a disadvantage. No significant amount of customer detail can be associated with each response without asking additional research questions, which would defeat the objective of a QR Code's quick and accessible format.

QR Codes are a useful alternative to large-scale feedback surveying or can offer a supplementary channel by which opinions and feedback can be collected alongside targeted customer surveying.

Also of interest: Always-On Survey.

QSR
Quick Service Restaurant
A retailer which serves only products that are produced within a very short space of time, typically take-away food items such as coffee, snack items or small meals.

Known mainly by the acronym QSR, these retailers are characterised by their small premises, lack of dine-in seating, high volume, high turnover customer bases and low-cost products.

Mainly franchised, branded QSR stores can number in the many thousands in some countries and are located within the highest concentration of populations, such as large towns and cities.

Measurement of service and customer satisfaction from QSR experiences has been of considerable interest to the broader CX research community in recent years. This is not only due to the growing number of QSR outlets but also because average customer visit times to such locations are typically extremely short. Therefore the delivery of positive customer experiences in such a short time frame is considered somewhat aspirational.

QUADRANT CHART
Quad Chart
A version of data chart representation which uses dots or points on a plotted graph, Quad charts are highly useful for understanding a wide distribution of data in a single view which in turn reveals outlying points of interest and focus. The format of quad charts is based on that of a Cartesian Plane with a distinct "cross-like" axis shape.

Whereas a traditional bar or line graph uses simple X (horizontal) and Y (vertical) axes to plot a single data point in the chart, Quad charts (implying the number four) break the chart plot area into four squares. The two X and Y-axis planes meet in the centre at intersection 0,0 to create the form of a cross and therefore four equal quadrants across the chart.

Data plotted on these axes can then be shown in either positive or negative relation to the axes themselves, appearing above or below the X-axis and either to the left or the right of the Y-axis in one of the quadrants of the chart.

The four quadrants can represent different areas of focus based on the data being plotted on the graph and what the axes are used to show. For example, where the X-axis shows "satisfaction" and the Y-axis shows "average spend", the consequent four quadrants can be used to show:
- Top left – Low satisfaction with a high average spend
- Top right – High satisfaction with a high average spend
- Bottom left – Low satisfaction with low average spend
- Bottom right – High satisfaction with low average spend

The value in CX of viewing data in this way is to help identify consistencies and inconsistencies within large data sets. For example, all "scores" taken from a feedback survey programme, plotted on a quad chart, can reveal where the large majority of responses might fall and additionally highlight the key areas for improvement.

QUALITATIVE RESEARCH
Qual research
A market research reference, Qualitative research involves a focus on language analysis, meaning and interpretation rather than data or numeric collection and interpretation. The etymology of the word qualitative stems back to the Latin word "qualitas", or "a quality, property or nature".

A Qualitative research project would involve the collection of spoken comments from respondents, transcribed from sources such as spoken interviews or recorded phone calls, into written words and then grouped and analysed for meaning and sentiment.

The objective of Qual research is to provide structure and codification to otherwise unstructured data. This is because unstructured data is typically much harder to analyse for thematic content and to identify the drivers a researcher would typically be looking for in customer experience analysis.

Traditional market research techniques used to analyse spoken comments include "Manual Coding", where comments are reviewed by researchers by eye and then grouped and "tagged" under different themes or categories. There are both advantages and problems with this approach. An advantage is that customer stories can be identified using the manual coding method. However, errors can easily be made in terms of identifying, coding and tagging comments, especially where large data sets are being read through by researchers by eye.

Very often market research professionals can be labelled colloquially as either "Quallies" or "Quanties", depending on individual specialisms or preferences for either research technique. Today's CX professional, however, needs experience, interest and an understanding of both Qual and Quant analysis as part of a balanced skillset.

Overall, Qualitative research is considered a vital element in the CX research mix as part of Voice of the Customer programmes which leverage analysis of written feedback and comments over hard metrics and numeric data.

Also of interest: Quantitative Research.

QUALITY ASSURANCE
QA
A series of methods in mainstream large scale production and customer service provision by which issues and quality problems are prevented and avoided.

The principles of QA are that companies adopting a QA system provide a range of measures, based on prior knowledge, assessments and education, that streamline production or service delivery processes and minimise risk, error and faults.

Specific product or channel applications of QA are known as Quality Control measures (or QC for short), and may be unique to that particular product or service.

Companies offering many products and services may therefore have a wide array of QC measures which form their overall QA strategy and plan.

Also of interest: Kaizen.

QUANTITATIVE RESEARCH
Quant Research
Any research methodology which collects mainly numeric and statistical data. The focus is on "quantifying" data, i.e. sizing and scaling results.

Used widely in traditional CX research, quantitative research can describe any methodology or approach where numeric information is collected. This can, therefore, apply to many different kinds of research, such as:

- Numeric scales
- Rating scales
- Counting and sizing exercises
- Graphing or plotting data points
- Analysis of sales data
- Customer base sizing
- Score comparisons and benchmarking

Since qualitative analysis is only focussed on numeric data, most statistical analysis methods and calculations can be applied to the results, and value and volumes can consequently be quantified.

Quantitative research excludes collection and analysis of qualitative data from non-numeric sources such as written or transcribed words, spoken audio, or video.

Also of interest: Qualitative Research.

QUOTA

A means of ensuring that data collected within research programmes and projects contains representative information from different groups to set amounts or percentages, known as Quotas.

Quota-setting within research programmes is important where there is a requirement to manage sample data according to specific population splits. Without set quotas, data that is collected in research may be widely variable, which may impact the overall results.

An example is that from a target total of 500 surveys, 300 responses should be from one customer type whilst the remaining 200 should be from another. Control parameters within the research phases should enable surveys to be targeted towards those specific customer types. Once enough surveys for each of those customer types has been achieved, that is when the research has met its quotas.

Projects may involve many individual quotas, adding to the complexity of the research phases, but which ensure consistency of measurement across a wide range of demographics.

Also of interest: Sample; Sampling.

R

RADIO BUTTON QUESTION

A form of survey question response format which is used in both paper-based and online research, where a subject is required to answer a question by making a single choice from a range of answer options. This is different from checkbox questions where more than one answer can be selected at the same time.

Radio buttons are presented to respondents as small circular buttons separated evenly in a horizontal scale. The number of buttons in the scale is determined by the length and type used in the question design, which can be numeric or worded (e.g. 1-3, 0-10, Yes/Maybe/No, etc.).

Respondents fill in the circle (on paper) or click on the relevant button (on a computer or mobile phone screen) which represents the answer they wish to select. They cannot select any other answer options.

Examples of where radio button format questions are used include:
• Simple "Yes" or "No" survey responses
• Customer Satisfaction and NPS answer scales
• A single choice in a list of options

Radio button questions are an ideal format to use when only

one answer from a range of options, or the most important or relevant answer option, is required.

Also of interest: Checkbox Question; Drop-Down Question; Multiple-Choice Question.

RAVING FAN

A term used in CX language today which describes a level of service received by a customer which is so good they become a strong brand or company advocate. It originated in popular culture by author Ken Blanchard in his 1993 book *"Raving Fans: A Revolutionary Approach to Customer Service"* co-authored with Sheldon Bowes.

The principles of generating Raving Fans is told in parable form in the book, which is based on a fictitious new manager's early days in a company that aspires to drive high levels of customer advocacy and consequently profitability. Several stages of achieving customer service excellence are worked through in sequence throughout the book, as the manager comes to form a new understanding and ideas of the principles behind these.

Having a customer base comprised of "Raving Fans" is an aspirational goal for many companies. Therefore the term appears regularly in company Customer Service charters, Road Maps, CX Strategy plans and general marketing communications.

It is closely aligned with measurement and metrics that show to what degree a company's customer base is already made of up Raving Fans (based on interpretation), and how to maintain continuously high levels of service-focus.

REAL-TIME FEEDBACK

Any research data which is collected and processed immediately, and made available for analysis and reporting purposes within a very short period after the research respondent has completed the feedback.

In modern CX programmes, real-time feedback is used to react quickly to situational issues which customers raise and which require expedient resolution, leading to Closed Loop feedback processes. The typical format of a real-time feedback survey will be sent via an automated system directly to the respondent, such as to a customer via an email-to-web survey invitation. Once the customer has replied to the survey and submitted their response, data servers collect the response, apply any filters or categorisation, and the result is made available immediately in a reporting resource such as an online CX Platform.

The majority of real-time feedback programmes and solutions operating today are not authentically real-time but are more like *near-real-time*. The reason for this is due to the delays that data processing can often cause. These include the application of filters, scanning for information which needs to be redacted (expletives, customer names, bank account numbers, etc.) and the potential backlog of data traffic moving in and out of the same server.

Similarly, some survey programmes are conducted through the distribution of research invitations in automated batches, and with encryption protocols being applied to the main results sets for maximum data security. Examples such as these cause further time delays and impact the real-time intention of such feedback programmes.

Real-time feedback is, by its nature, in complete contrast to more traditional research methods which involve much longer lead times and more manual intervention. However, real-time feedback management is growing increasingly popular among companies who understand the value of reacting rapidly to customer sentiment and in turn helps CX professionals to retain a live "pulse" of the latest programme information.

Also of interest: Closed Loop; CX Platform.

REGRESSION ANALYSIS

A form of statistical analysis which attempts to establish the relationship between different types of variables in research data.

The term regression, with regard to this analytical technique, was first used by Francis Galton in the 19th century and concerned his examination of growth patterns in human sample groups. He found that the average height of tall ancestors "regressed" towards a normal average, and could be distributed on a graph or chart. Similar patterns are often seen in data analysis of this type in other areas, hence the use of the term.

The variables used in regression analysis are dependent variables and independent variables; in short, values which depend on and influence each other. The outcomes of the relationships between these variables can be visually represented on graphs, where X and Y axes are used to plot the independent and dependent variables respectively.

Distribution of data points on regression graphs may roughly represent the direction of a diagonal line, gradually rising from left to right. Consequently, a straight line can be plotted on these graphs to show the average pattern of results and is called Linear Regression, the most common form of regression analysis.

Regression analysis is particularly useful for CX researchers who are attempting to establish the distribution of factors which have cause and impact on experiences, e.g. events which influence loyalty, satisfaction, recommendation, repeat purchasing, etc.

One of the drawbacks of this type of analytical technique is that it assumes that a relationship between data variables exists and that this relationship is straight-line and therefore plottable, which is not always true. In these cases, other more advanced variations of regression analysis can be deployed, which account for greater complexities in the relationships between data sets.

RELATIONSHIP NPS
rNPS; Strategic NPS
Net Promoter Score results from research on many customer interactions with brands, companies or products over time are known as relationship NPS surveys; often rNPS for short.

rNPS measurement is conducted strategically in that respondents will be asked to offer ratings of their likelihood to recommend a brand, service or product based on many experiences over a long period. This is very different from Transactional NPS or tNPS, which asks respondents to provide the same rating but on only one very recent experience. The period of rNPS measurement is not fixed but assumes that more than interaction has occurred between the respondent and company or service provider over time.

The NPS question wording is adapted for rNPS surveys as follows:

"Based on the experiences you have had [insert time frame, e.g. this year] how likely is it that you would recommend this company, product or service to a friend or colleague?"

Consequently, because of the long period respondents are being asked to consider, rNPS can reveal factors and drivers which are unique to this type of NPS questioning, such as:
- A mixture of good and bad experiences
- More respondent consideration, less emotion
- Generalisations rather than specific event details
- Lack of specific event recall
- External factors such as company reputation, brand health and media influence

Many companies who collect NPS across many channels utilise

both rNPS and tNPS and see and understand the key differences between the two. As a result, rNPS is suited well for research with subjects who are harder to reach and are contacted less frequently. These might include business or corporate customers, individuals whose affairs are managed by a proxy or through a 3rd party, or private individuals such as wealth banking customers.

rNPS is also well suited for group discussions and panel interviews, where general impressions and general likelihood to recommend can be gained from a broad range of research subjects at once.

Also of interest: Net Promoter Score; Relationship Survey; tNPS.

RELATIONSHIP SURVEY

A form of research which measures and collects information about relationships between customers and companies, brands, product or service providers.

Relationship surveys are typically broad by design and capture information from respondents based on multiple interactions with brands over long periods. The methodologies used for relationships surveys can include long-form online surveys, short-form rNPS surveys, personal interviews either by telephone (CATI) or online (CAWI), paper-based research and more. These research methods enable a higher volume of questions to be asked. They may balance both quantitative and qualitative question types to capture respondent opinion of overall loyalty and other relationship factors.

Relationship surveys are not well suited to high-frequency surveying and are often conducted at frequencies such as quarterly, half-yearly or annually.

They are the opposite of transactional surveys and are not necessarily triggered by or tied to a single event. Instead, they are strategic in nature, where aggregated outcomes from the research project provide a strategic view of customer relationships based on a fixed sample of respondents.

Depending on the design of the initial research questionnaire, relationship surveys can perform several functions. They can provide information about the drivers behind various loyalty factors, offer an overview of services and product quality, can include a high level of general opinion and are an excellent source of customer verbatim commentary.

Also of interest: Relationship NPS.

REMOTE SERVICING

The ability for company employees to continue to provide customer servicing and support whilst working away from a company headquarters or office building, often securely connecting to company systems over the internet using computers and mobile devices.

Employees of companies are required to operate away from fixed headquarters locations in many different ways, for example:
- Customer service employees who handle calls at home
- Sales agents visiting clients in the field
- Personal trainers offering video fitness classes to students)

IBM was one of the first companies to experiment with the positive impact of remote working by enabling five of their employees to work from home in the late 1970s, and by the early 1980s had expanded those numbers to allow a much greater workforce to be based remotely.

CX has been impacted significantly by a steady increase in remote working possibilities, driven by changes in engagements between companies and customers, which have become more virtual over time.

An example is where customers who make telephone enquiries

to companies may not have any awareness that their calls are being handled by a remote employee based at home. Meanwhile, the access those employees have to home comforts and conveniences is seen as beneficial in terms of both their experience delivery to customers and overall job satisfaction.

REPRESENTATIVE SAMPLE
A selection of research results, such as survey responses from target subjects, which is considered accurately representative of a much broader base.

If a smaller research sample demonstrates similar outcomes to those that might be expected from a broader research exercise, then it can be said to be "representative". This may include factors such as an even distribution of respondents from different types and categories such as gender, age, income, preferences, etc.

Confidence in representative sampling is important for companies and organisations who have allocated budgets to their research strategies and cannot afford to or have the available resources to conduct broad-range measurement.

Also of interest: Quota; Sample; Sampling.

RESEARCH
The investigation and discovery of new information, using a wide variety of methods, intended to answer questions, address hypotheses and reveal unknown insights.

Research forms the bedrock of many CX strategies and programmes since the outcomes of CX research enable strategic decisions and choices to be made to improve overall customer experiences.

Also of interest: Feedback; Interview; Survey.

RESEARCH PANEL
See: Panel

RESOLUTION TIME
The time that is taken by an organisation to address and resolve customer enquiries, complaints or issues. This may be in terms of minutes, hours, days or otherwise – depending entirely on the service model an organisation offers and the type of products and services it sells.

Resolution time is typically seen as a measurable factor in Customer Services departments and Operations teams. It is closely linked to other similar Contact Centre-based measures such as First Time Resolution (FTR) and On-Time Resolution (OTR).

Overall Resolution Times, and the outcomes of resolving a high volume of customer enquiries successfully, are often expressed as an average (the average time taken to resolve enquiries), a percentage (of all enquiries resolved within an SLA-based time frame) or as a straight number (the total number of enquiries resolved within an SLA-based time frame).

As with FCR and OTR, companies who resolve a high number of customer enquiries within the shortest time frames possible often seek to correlate this with levels of customer satisfaction and advocacy.

RESPONDENT
In research terms, a respondent is an individual who has completed some form of interview or survey, either with an interviewer or using automated technology, the results of which may be combined with other responses to form an overall picture of CX.

Respondent types and targeting will depend entirely on the research being undertaken, its objectives and delivery method.

RESPONSE BIAS
See: Bias

RESPONSE FATIGUE
Survey Fatigue
Response fatigue refers to the factors which might cause a research subject or survey respondent to lose interest in the completion of a research exercise, potentially leaving their response incomplete.

The reasons respondents become fatigued with research exercises, surveys or interviews include the following:
- Too many questions are asked or are repeated
- The questionnaire takes too long to complete
- The research subject matter and questions are boring
- The research is no longer relevant and is too long after the respondent's initial experience
- Surveys are sent to subjects too often
- Respondents are not rewarded for their efforts

Response fatigue is a major consideration during the phases of research and questionnaire design. It is, therefore, a key factor when research agencies or CX professionals design customer interviews, surveys or feedback forms.

Many of the root causes of response fatigue, such as those listed above, can be mitigated through adopting the principles of good research design. Some of these principles are as follows:
- Ensuring the purpose of the research is for experience improvement purposes, not an attempt to market or sell products and services
- Ensuring the research survey or questionnaire is not unnecessarily long
- Avoiding repetitive, unengaging or confusing research questions
- Ensuring the research questions are relevant to the respondent

- Sending the research invitation soon after an event to ensure accurate recall
- Avoiding issues with research or interviewer/interviewee technique, conduct or language barrier
- Avoiding too many open-ended comments sections

Well-tested, relevant and compact questionnaires which include dynamic branching that are sent to subjects in a timely manner are likely to yield far higher engagement and response rates than otherwise.

Therefore avoidance of response fatigue is an important factor in ensuring the maximum number of respondents complete the research in which they are invited to participate.

Also of interest: Drop-Out Rate.

RESPONSE RATE

The rate of completion of research surveys by respondents, typically expressed as a percentage of the total invitations sent.

There is no set or agreed optimal survey response rate, although achieving as many survey responses, and therefore as high a rate as possible, is often the desired outcome within CX research.

Methods by which surveys are issued to respondents have a significant impact on the final response rate, and the following are examples of response rates which may be seen:
- Email-to-web surveys: 10% or <
- SMS "ping pong" surveys: 25% or <
- Web intercept surveys: 1-5%
- CATI: 80-100% (but a vastly reduced final quota compared with surveying methods such as those above)

The examples above come with *heavy* caveats, as many factors can have an impact on the response rate seen. For example, the circumstance and context of the survey invite request (feedback or a complaint), the engagement channel the survey subject refers to (store experience, online experience, phone experience) the industry within which surveying takes place, etc.

In some circumstances in CX research, response rates are not advisable as a critical indicator of the success of the project. This is because some methodologies are expected to achieve high response rates anyway (e.g. CATI, where researchers make repeat calls to target respondents until close to 100% is reached). Another reason is where the focus of the research project is instead on qualitative outputs rather than high volumes of completed surveys.

Response rates are one of several measures used to manage the process of execution of a CX research project, feedback programme, project or study; others include sample management and achievement of survey quota.

Also of interest: Drop-Out Rate; Quota; Sample; Sampling.

RETURN ON INVESTMENT
ROI
A term which is used very widely in modern business but in a CX context refers directly to the net financial gain of investing in CX initiatives.

A clear ROI is commonly a principal goal for companies investing in CX programmes, as the high costs of executing CX research and management often requires leadership support and agreement for funding to be allocated or continued.

Where CX strategies are shown in the form of a company maturity curve, ROI is typically shown at the mature end of the curve. In this light, ROI is seen as a vital part of any business case that CX professionals should expect to write and potentially represent several times in their business to secure widespread stakeholder support.

Examples of ROI commonly sought by companies executing CX initiatives include:

- Upturn or increase in customer spending based on improvements put in place which in turn have been gained from outcomes of the CX research initiative or programme
- Increases in customer loyalty and general satisfaction measurements included as part of the CX research programme
- The costs of the research programme or service pays for itself by way of increased company profitability

It is seen that providing a clear linkage between the improvements made directly from CX insights and increased company profitability is a compelling reason for profit-focused board members to agree to current and future CX funding.

rNPS
See: Relationship NPS

ROAD MAP
A clearly stated or visualised pathway towards a strategic objective or series of CX goals. These are typically included at the top level of CX strategic design, where stakeholders in the process can discuss and agree with the direction and define the steps to be taken to achieve a company's overall goals.

CX road maps are often put into a visual format for cascade across organisations, deliberately shareable and intended to ensure a clear understanding of activities at a high level across different groups. These can be based on the format of a linear timeline, with key actions and milestones shown along the timeline.

Examples include graphical maps, infographics, PowerPoint visuals, flow charts, Journey Maps and many other visualisations.

Successful CX road maps are not just a long list of projects to deliver and activities to undertake. They should clearly show the key objectives leadership groups have agreed together, the points at which it is expected each goal will be achieved and the positive impacts associated with each achievement. This is whether the agreed objectives are financial, cultural, operational or otherwise.

S

SAAS
Software-as-a-Service

Any complete or packaged system or application which is based in the cloud and made available to end-users through online or virtual access. SaaS software is not licenced and sold in the same way as Hosted or On-Premise software, as it is essentially "rented" by clients, and the technology resides on virtual servers which can be located anywhere in the world.

Examples of SaaS applications for CX include:
- Customer record keeping: SaaS CRM system
- Customer management: SaaS agent desktop software
- Customer surveying: SaaS CX Platform

SaaS software is the most popular and most widely deployed form of computer application in respect of CX use. It offers many advantages, including instant online access and enhanced data protection and privacy features. Additionally, SaaS customers benefit from regular version updates and feature additions released on a scheduled basis together with ongoing maintenance and technical support.

SaaS differs from the more general area of Cloud software and computing; the latter which describes a broad range of online systems and tools which may be used as various components to provide a complete service. SaaS is a more specific, tailored and dedicated package of online tools such as the examples listed above.

In some industries and countries, SaaS applications are not preferred nor permitted due to either local data retention and transfer laws or the preference for managing customer data only using On-Premise software.

Also of interest: Cloud Software; Hosted Software; On-Premise.

SAMPLE
A market research reference which describes both the intended volume of results which will be gathered during an upcoming research programme (target sample) and the resulting data gathered (final sample). Sample subjects are, therefore, those included in the intended sample group.

Sample control is important in traditional research for several reasons, such as the avoidance of exhausting available target sample groups too quickly and managing costs associated with the research process.

Also of interest: Bias; Quota; Sampling; Segmentation.

SAMPLING
The process of defining and generating a sample target for use in research projects and activities.

Also of interest: Quota; Sample.

SCORECARD
A series of scores, KPIs or other metrics which are used in company management to track a wide range of performance and operational factors for individuals, teams, departments, business units and company overall.

The practice of devising a company performance Scorecard to track a range of key business KPIs has also led to the current concept of incorporating CX performance into such reporting.

The format of a Scorecard is typically represented in a way that different key measurable elements carry a weighted or "balanced" importance. For example, a multi-part grid or Dashboard showing KPIs, running totals or tracking metrics. These may or may not be equal, based on the respective importance of each element.

In recent years, CX as a metric or a measure in varying formats has been included by some companies in their overall Performance Scorecard, alongside more traditional KPIs such as sales revenues, profitability, employee engagement and so on.

Opinion remains divided on the success of including CX measures in Scorecards in the same way that other "hard" measures can be tracked. For example, sales revenues can be reported as a definite number. In contrast, a single number for CX cannot easily be calculated or shown unless a quantifiable metric such as NPS or C-SAT is being used.

Many companies use CX metrics as part of a Scorecard to reward and remunerate teams and individuals based on their performance against a target. Again, this remains in dispute among companies who believe this creates a number-chasing culture at the expense of actually listening to and acting on feedback.

Employees measured on CX in this way often also state that it is the measure that they have the least control over and is perhaps an unfair inclusion as part of a Scorecard comprised of otherwise hard metrics.

To mitigate these challenges, in recent years some companies have used a representative CX number as a means to "unlock" reward and recognition at given levels from their own Scorecards, but only if all other metrics and performance criteria are also met.

Also of interest: KPI.

SEASONALITY
The impact of recurring events throughout the annual year which might affect CX research outcomes. Analysis of seasonality can reveal much by way of insight when examining what happens to research results over a period. Trended analysis of seasonality can include how key tracking metrics such as NPS or customer satisfaction are impacted by recurring public holidays and due to planned sporting, music or public events, for example.

Unanticipated factors can also impact experience outcomes considerably – more so than known seasonal events since organisations have very little chance to prepare for them and therefore mitigate the effects. These might include a wide range of examples such as financial market fluctuations, unpredicted weather patterns, political activities such as snap elections or protests, flash sales by companies, illness and disease, mass corporate redundancies, etc.

One of the industries where seasonal impact can be seen most prominently in customer experience research is retail, where regular research programmes which track performance or feedback show peaks and troughs at periods such as those given above. Seasonal impact in all its possible forms is, therefore, commonly used to provide context and backdrop when analysing experience research outcomes.

SECONDARY RESEARCH
Desk research
A market research reference which involves the analysis of existing research data without the need to conduct further research to refresh or generate any new data sets.

Examples of secondary or desk research include using existing data from a variety of sources such as databases and reports and actively researching existing public resources such as the internet.

Secondary research is often used to either support or refute the findings of Primary research, especially when collecting and analysing information gathered over time.

Also of interest: Primary Research.

SEGMENTATION

A form of analysis which separates research results and groups based on their types or characteristics. Segmenting data results helps researchers to understand commonalities between those groups.

Examples in CX include the segmentation of customers into buying types or Personas, which in turn helps companies to market and service more effectively to those customers and increase sales, loyalty, advocacy and other factors.

Typical forms of CX segmentation analysis include groupings such as:
- Age, gender and other personal profile details
- Geographical location
- Purchasing behaviours and spending patterns
- Income and savings
- Account or product types
- Values and attitudes

Segmentation has been used for many years in market research as the basis by why customers can be categorised.
Consequently, companies can address their services and needs in specific ways.

Also of interest: Persona; Population Study; Psychographic Segmentation; Sample; Sampling.

SELF-SERVICE

The methods by which customers serve themselves and address their own enquiries through using automated services such as information resources, software applications, websites and AI.

Self-service capabilities have existed for some time in many industries, an example of which is mobile banking. In such cases, customers are in control of their activities, product interactions, payment schedules; can set up, pay for and interact with new products and services; and access FAQs sources or virtual assistants such as ChatBots.

Whilst self-service is advantageous in many ways for both service providers and customers, it is essential to enable seamless links between self-service capabilities and human representatives to address more complex enquiries and activities.

SENTIMENT ANALYSIS

See: Text Analytics

SENTIMENT CLOUD

An advanced version of a Word Cloud, but with the distinct difference of showing words in the cloud that are based on the sentiment associated with analysed words and phrases. This is compared with standard Word Clouds, which only show the frequency of occurrence of a word in a data set.

Sentiment clouds are used to provide an attractive visual representation of customer sentiment based on analysis of data, taken from the same sources as standard Word Clouds such as online posts, survey verbatim and speech transcribed into text.

Unlike standard Word Clouds, however, which simply count and represent words or phrase occurrence, sentiment clouds show data that has been processed by software with Natural Language Processing capabilities such as Text Analytics applications. The word sentiment can typically be "tuned" as per the context of the sentence and phrase it occurs in by researchers who manage the data set, within the controls offered by the text analytics software. These are then visualised within the clouds in text colours such as red (negative sentiment), yellow (neutral sentiment) and green (positive sentiment). Each of these colour representations can be based on scales available within the text analytics software (e.g. 7, 5 or 3-point negative to positive sentiment), and the overall sentiment of the word(s) determines the colours that are shown.

Depending on software in use, sentiment clouds can be featured in CX reporting Dashboards alongside charts and graphs showing key CX metrics as a compelling visualisation of overall trending customer opinion.

Also of interest: Dashboard; Machine Learning; Natural Language Processing; Text Analytics; Word Cloud.

SENTIMENT TAG
A method of creating a link to a specific word, part of a sentence or a whole phrase within a set of data in a text analytics application and attributing a sentiment value to it.

Sentiment tags are used in text and Sentiment Analysis to identify sections of unstructured data. A positive or negative value will be attributed to a selection of unstructured data, such as an online comment or a transcribed sound file, by the AI algorithm that is built into the analysis programme. This is done through word and sentence recognition which is either pre-programmed or machine-learned.

Each tagged phrase will then be included in results analysis when filters matching that tag are selected and applied. For example, only customer feedback comments that were tagged at 3 out of 5 on a positive sentiment scale.

Also of interest: Text Analytics.

SERVICE TICKET
A single case or record which is raised by or on behalf of a customer when making a complaint, raising an issue or making an enquiry.

Service Tickets are used in CX case management to create unique electronic records of the information required to manage dialogue and conduct resolutions with each customer. These are typically submitted using an online template, with a fixed number of fields including necessary customer contact information, the nature of the enquiry and any survey ratings which initially triggered the creation of the ticket.

The processes of resolving service tickets are usually bound by internal SLAs so that a company should make every attempt to close tickets with customer satisfaction within agreed timeframes.

Also of interest: Closed Loop.

SINGLE-SIGN-ON
SSO
A method by which individual users and employees, usually in large companies with widely distributed workforces, can log into various computer systems and programmes through one authenticated and secure process.

SSO enables either remote or onsite users to conveniently access various programmes, applications and networked systems with a single entry of their username and password. For SSO to be made possible, these different programmes are connected through a centralised platform and to data warehousing facilities.

SSO is useful in CX where it offers the ability for employees to access 3rd party applications such as CX Platforms, survey management systems and reporting Dashboards that are integrated with company networks.

Many benefits exist with SSO, including the convenience of access to connected systems, reduction of log-in fatigue, minimisation of the loss or forgetting of log-in credentials and traceability of user access across different systems.

SIX SIGMA
Lean Six Sigma

A managerial concept adopted by many companies worldwide to help streamline and maximise organisational efficiencies. The name "six sigma" is a reference to a statistical model which produces a graphical representation of bell curve, on which the different "sigmas" are shown at various distances from the mean (average).

Six Sigma originates from the combination of a variety of process improvements related to manufacturing. Its roots are in Lean manufacturing, made famous by the production processes adopted by Toyota in Japan in the 1950s and the continuous improvement methodologies of Kaizen.

Lean Six Sigma in its own right was adapted from these original principles, popularised by companies such as Motorola in the 1980s, and has today become an aligned set of business principles which aim to:
- Reduce unnecessary wastage (Lean principles)
- Improve the quality of production outputs by removing defects and stabilising consistency

Lean Six Sigma principles relate beneficially to CX, where customer opinion and feedback through research impacts the development of improvements to products and services in an organisation.

Customer research is therefore considered an important part of a Lean Six Sigma process, and many CX professionals are also therefore Lean Six Sigma trained. The stages of seniority regarding Six Sigma experience are graded belts in the order of Yellow Belt (most junior) through Green, Black and finally Master Black Belt (most senior).

Also of interest: Kaizen.

SLIDING QUESTION
A format of survey question response, designed for touch screens such as those on mobile phones and laptop devices, where respondents use a finger to move a slider along a fixed line to provide a rating selection.

Online surveys can be designed with a range of answer options, and sliding questions are used most effectively where ratings along a fixed line do not need to be shown. The respondent simply moves the slider along the line and places it where they feel is appropriate. Usually, both ends of the scale are labelled so that respondents know which represents low and which is high.

A granularity of responses can also be collected using sliding scales. For example, rather than only having fixed response points along a line, the respondent may choose to stop the slider at a point which indicates any number within a wide range (e.g. 0-100), not just at fixed data points within a limited range (e.g. 0-10).

Sliding scales are also seen as a way to enhance respondent survey engagement, providing an alternative to standard radio buttons and checkbox formats.

SMS GATEWAY
Technology which enables SMS messages to be sent across mobile networks to customers on their mobile handsets.

CX companies conducting research using SMS, such as ping-pong surveys or SMS-to-web surveys, require SMS gateway connections to allow their surveys to be received on customer mobile phones.

These can be provided by surveying technology companies and mobile aggregators, allowing researchers to survey subjects in any language, in any country.

Also of interest: Ping-Pong Survey; SMS Survey.

SMS SURVEY

Conducted via handset phone text messaging services, SMS is short for "Short Message Service". Within Customer Experience across the past 20 or so years, SMS has become popular in gaining immediate post-transaction feedback at high volumes. SMS surveys are typically delivered right after a customer's experience, such as a phone call to a Customer Service Contact Centre or completion of a booked appointment for a car service.

The value of SMS in customer research is that response rates can be much higher than other survey types; for example, SMS surveys can achieve around a 25% response rate compared with low single-digit % for email-to-web surveys. This does depend, however, on timing, context, number of questions, etc.

Another benefit of SMS in research is that, by using appropriate technology such as a connected survey management platform, SMS surveys can be triggered almost immediately after the customer experience has ended, so that feedback can be captured "in the moment".

However, there are some restrictions with SMS as a research format. Global rules, born out of the work done by GSM (Global System for Mobile Communications) in the mid-1980s, determined that mobile networks could only carry a limited amount of additional data alongside mobile phone calls. Thus the 160 character limit for SMS messages was set and remains in place today.

The impact on SMS research is that each message in the entire "conversation" must be worded to no more than 160 characters, including spaces. Too many survey questions will result in too many SMS messages back and forth between company and customer, possibly resulting in incomplete surveys due to response fatigue.

Additionally, there is a cost implication. Each SMS survey typically consumes a "credit" which is charged by the mobile network back to the company conducting the SMS research. Many SMS survey questions and responses between company and customers can accumulate quickly, and it is considered best practice for the researching company to cover the cost of all of these.

For these reasons, SMS surveying is considered a very straightforward and accessible methodology for gaining real-time customer feedback results with higher response rates than some other survey channels but is at the same time restricted in scope and depth of research due to character limits and potential high overall costs.

Also of interest: Ping-Pong Survey; SMS Gateway; SMS-to-Web Survey.

SMS-TO-WEB SURVEY

A survey invitation which is sent to a subject via SMS messaging using mobile handsets, containing a weblink which will take the respondent to a website survey when clicked.

This methodology for inviting subjects to complete surveys is a useful alternative to email-to-web surveys and can help to bolster response rates for research and feedback programmes. In the cases where email survey invites may have been missed or ignored by respondents, SMS invitations are more effective, as they are sent to mobile phones over mobile networks. They are therefore visible to respondents without an internet connection to an email program.

SMS-to-web invitations can also be used as a reminder methodology, sent a short time after an initial email-to-web invite. This approach, once again, can attract additional responses from target recipients.

SMS-to-web invitations are bound by length protocols, just like any other form of SMS. This is a maximum of 160 characters per message (including spaces), so many companies sending SMS survey invitations to customers use a programme to shorten the character length of the web link in the message body. This is known as a "tiny url" and can avoid SMS-to-web invitations running over to more than one SMS to each recipient.

The capability to send SMS-to-web invites to customers requires connections to mobile networks and, therefore, a reliance on a dependable and up-to-date contact base of customers. Many CX Platforms have components which enable researchers to design, send and report on SMS-to-web invites alongside the design and management of linked website surveys.

Also of interest: SMS Gateway; SMS Survey.

SOCIAL LISTENING
See: Social Media Analysis

SOCIAL MEDIA
Any method of communication which enables users to share information online with an internet audience. This is typically through the format of content posted on websites and through dedicated mobile applications such as community platforms and can include opinions, news articles, reviews, ratings, videos, documentaries, public posts and comments.

SOCIAL MEDIA ANALYSIS
The process of examining and investigating content and data from social media sources for insight and intelligence, and to

enable forward action.

Social media websites and apps in all forms have become a vital series of engagement channels between companies and their customers today. The rise of social internet activity and the possibility of direct dialogue with companies has led to a substantial and rich base of data for mining customer sentiment and intelligence without the need for direct surveying or interview-based research.

Companies who specialise in social media analysis tools have seen their uptake and usage explode in the last decade, and many of these software applications leverage Natural Language Processing (NLP), Machine Learning and Sentiment Analysis to provide aggregated insight to users.

Many companies have set up and employed specialist teams to manage social media content and engagement channels, including the development of relationships with key social media influencers. Social media engagement with customers has also been operationalised in many other companies, where Customer Service departments provide dedicated support through agents managing chat and dialogue with customers on websites such as Twitter and Facebook.

Alongside other methods of researching customers such as surveys and interviews, social media channels have become a primary source for CX programme insight, management and change.

SPEECH ANALYTICS
Voice Analytics
A process or software application which analyses human voice patterns such as recorded phone calls for information.

Many technology companies have developed sophisticated Speech Analytics software which is now is used by organisations who primarily engage with their customers through phone calls to Contact Centres. Before such technology was made available, voice recordings of phone calls would have been manually tagged and analysed using a lengthy and error-prone human listening and checking process.

Speech Analytics involves the use of automated speech recognition software which identifies single words, key phrases, acronyms, references and emotional reaction in spoken dialogue. The software, which typically has off-the-shelf capabilities and standard word taxonomies built into the application, can be fine-tuned for the purpose it is being used for as well as the particular industry sector in which it is being deployed.

Data from analysed calls can be visualised in the form of online Dashboards and quantitative reports, which highlighted frequency and occurrence, trending themes and levels of emotional reaction.

Words can also be transcribed from audio into written form so that Text Analytics can be applied. However, many users have mixed opinion about whether audio-based language can and should be analysed and treated in the same way as written language since they are two very distinct methods of human communication.

Many Speech Analytics software packages available today can recognise multiple languages and are therefore deployed across different operating markets by some companies to assess the levels of service they provide and listen to customer feedback from different cultures and geographies.

The use cases for Speech Analytics in CX are extensive. They can encompass mandatory compliance checking, avoidance of risk, standardisation of service delivery, benchmarking, training, CX management and feedback analysis, among others.

SPSS
Originally: Statistical Package for the Social Sciences
Later: Statistical Product and Service Solutions
SPSS is a popular computer software package which has been used for many years in the market research industry to enable the analysis of large amounts of statistical data.

It was created and initially programmed by the developers Norman Nie, Dale Bent and Hadlai Hull in 1968 and has gone through many iterations and updates. Eventually, SPSS was acquired by IBM in 2009 and is now known as IBM SPSS Statistics (v27 at time of writing).

The package is considered particularly useful by researchers due to its set of structured models and pre-programmed reporting features, including straight statistical data analysis tools and predictive modelling. It has a dedicated user interface (visually similar to spreadsheets and databases) and enables developers with knowledge of Python and R computer programming languages to customise and adapt the software to their requirements.

The software also enables the testing of hypotheses and assumptions based on historical data analysis.

CX researchers have made use of SPSS by analysing large sets of data results from survey programmes, creating statistical models for different customer types and analysing customer buying behaviours.

STAR RATING
A form of rating scale question where numbered points along a scale are replaced by stars in a horizontal line, with low and high values indicated. Respondents select the star which best represents their answer.

Similar to emoji scales, Star Ratings are offered as a novel alternative to standard rating scale questions in feedback surveys.

As an attractive visual trigger for respondents to choose a star based on the experience they had, Star Ratings can offer effective high volume data capture, but little by way of insight behind why respondents make their selections.

Typical formats include 3 to 5 coloured stars as seen in mobile or web surveys, and star ratings can often be seen in examples such as surveys following holiday travel, ratings on social media sites and feedback following usage of websites and conference call facilities.

STRATEGIC NPS
See: Relationship NPS

STRATIFIED SAMPLE
A method of dividing a sample group intended for research into subgroups, creating "stratification" (layers) of groups within an overall research programme. Each group may be selected for variations on the research methodology, questions and objectives according to their type and suitability.

Stratifying sample data in this way enables granularity of research focus and measurement as opposed to a blanket approach taken across an entire sample group. It also allows for adequate representation of subgroups within the final results, avoiding misrepresentation and overweighting.

Also of interest: Quota; Sample; Sampling.

STRUCTURED DATA
Data that is in a recognisable and format, consistent across different data sets, and can therefore be used in standard forms, files and programs.

Examples of structured, consistent data are:

- Bank account numbers with the same number of digits (e.g. 8)
- First and last names
- Postcodes/Zip Codes
  ...and so on

The advantage of structured data to end-users is that it is predictable and consistent. Therefore management frameworks, filing systems, and reporting can be built around data where the format is recognisable.

Structured data is the opposite of unstructured data, which obeys no set order or consistency in terms of length, type or predictability.

Also of interest: Unstructured Data.

STUDY

A general term used to describe a single piece of research in any subject or area. Root usage of the term refers to when subjects were "studied".

A legacy market research reference, the term "study" has become outdated in modern research when describing ongoing CX programmes. It is also now used less commonly when describing continuous measurement programmes such as real-time Voice of the Customer surveying.

SURVEY

A type of research in which one or more questions can be sent via a wide variety of methods to a group of subjects who return their completed responses individually. The results are gathered together and form the basis of a complete research sample for the research project in question.

Surveys are typically sent to respondents who self-complete their responses, most often electronically. This differs from interviews, which are conducted in person or via telephone where a researcher documents the respondent's answers.

Also of interest: Feedback; Interview; Research.

SYNDICATED RESEARCH

A method of researching on a large scale, usually within a specific industry, segment or country, followed by the production of a report with the intent to sell on the open market. Participating companies who agree to their data to be included in the research gain the advantage of being able to compare their results on a like-for-like basis with their nearest competitors.

In CX, syndicated reporting often takes the form of a research programme with specific questions targeted to individuals or organisations within a given industry sector or geography, and then provision of a report showing all results and comparing these outcomes against Norms and Benchmarks tables. Data downloads and presentations often accompany the reports, and client buyers may be able to conduct their own analysis based on access to the raw data.

Large scale market research agencies often run such syndicated reports due to their wide size and coverage and these are commonly made available for purchase either ad hoc or as part of an ongoing contract or subscription. Market sectors covered by syndicated reports available today include financial services, automotive and retail and the format of reporting is data-led with high-level conclusions typically offered by agencies against the results.

Due to the size, scope, variability and initial cost (to the operating agency) of each report, these are run infrequently and typically are made available quarterly, bi-annually or annually.

The methodology and metrics used to capture respondent information can vary by market research agency and can include methods such as CATI, CAPI and CAWI as well as Focus Groups, usage of Panel and Communities and also real-time web survey-based feedback.

A key advantage of Syndicated reporting for the CX buyer is the ability to access a broad range of relevant industry information quickly and with raw data to hand to make generic analysis possible.

A drawback, however, is that the results are, by their nature, high level, and often do not drill down into specific themes which in turn does not necessarily enable strategic decision making or offer competitor insight.

Syndicated reporting is therefore used primarily by companies as a tracker and rank report of own performance versus immediate competitors in the same sector or country.

T

TACTICAL NPS
See: Transactional NPS

TAXONOMY
The classification of words and references into groups and sets according to their types.

Taxonomies are a vital component of Text Analytics software functionality which utilises taxonomies of various types to organise unstructured data into structured groups. This can be based on simple word recognition alone or using advanced capabilities such as sentiment tagging.

Also of interest: Sentiment Tag; Text Analytics.

TETRAPHOBIA
Quadrophobia
In some cultures in Asia, avoidance of the use of the number four due to superstitious reasons. The closest proxy in Western cultures is a superstition of the number thirteen; however, tetraphobia in Asia is more commonplace and pronounced.

Tetraphobia, or quadrophobia as it is sometimes known, is most prevalent in Asian cultures due to the pronounced sound of the word "four" being very similar to the sound of the word for "death". This is in Indo-Chinese and Japanese root languages in particular. An example is the Mandarin Chinese versions of both words which sound almost identical when pronounced: "*sì*". The similarities are less strong where dialects and regional accents vary.

This causes enough impact in some Asian markets for the number four to be avoided in relation to house prices, hotel room doors and floors, product numbering, monetary systems and telephone numbers.

This does have an impact on some metric, numeric, scale and quantification-based CX research work and customer surveying conducted in Asia, although not substantially. Occasionally, fewer responses of four can be seen on metric scales such as NPS; or fewer respondents choose four of anything when answering research questions.

TEXT ANALYTICS
TA; Text Mining; Verbatim Analytics
Software which enables large volumes of unstructured data to be analysed for meaning, sentiment and forward action.

Use of Text Analytics, or TA for short, has increased in popularity among CX researchers in recent years as a considerable advancement on Manual Coding, which was the only available option before the process of TA was computerised.

TA makes use of advanced functions such as Natural Language Processing and Machine Learning to analyse large volumes of unstructured text-based data. The technology makes this process a far more practical solution with a far higher accuracy rate compared with Manual Coding, which is conducted by humans by eye.

The sources for TA data can be any unstructured data such as:
- Customer verbatim in surveys
- Transcribed audio or video dialogue

- Agent notes from records of customer calls and conversations
- Social media comments and reviews
- Closed Loop resolution notes from employees

...and any other form of written words that are digitally transcribed or scanned.

The TA engine will assess a range of data using either off-the-shelf models or customised models to examine words within a given context. For example, words and language which may have specific meaning within financial services may not have the same meaning in general language. An example of this is the meaning of the word "charge" which in banking terms means a penalty fee.

For this reason, TA engines are typically built using different taxonomies within which the meanings behind certain words and phrases are specific to that industry model. In this way, different TA taxonomies can be applied to data from specific scenarios so that the analysis is more accurate and contextual.

Once data has been uploaded into the TA application, a variety of AI, Machine Learning and NLP processes may be applied to the data set to achieve several things, depending on how advanced the TA engine is:

- Categorise data
- Segment data based on attributes
- Present the most commonly occurring words and references
- Search for specific words and references, known as "Text Mining"
- Highlight trending themes based on historical comparison
- Allocate sentiment scores to words and phrases

The latter point, where sentiment scores are applied to text, is one of the most powerful ways of examining unstructured data for meaning and action. This goes above and beyond simple "word counting" even at a large scale as TA technology can "tag" words and phrases with sentiment, sometimes mixed, to help identify the root cause behind customer comments and how companies can improve services and products and drive higher satisfaction.

A simple example of Sentiment Analysis applied to a customer comment might be as follows:

> "I _enjoyed_ my restaurant experience. _The food was great,_ although the _service was a little slow_. The _toilets weren't very clean,_ but this didn't detract from _a good experience overall._"

The customer comment above can be said to have mixed sentiment, shown where underlined. There are aspects of the comment which reflect a good/positive experience, some elements that are indifferent and some that are poor. Using sentiment tagging, the TA engine would apply a positive, neutral or negative tag to relevant sections of the text, and in the cases of some TA solutions offering the research user the ability to "tune" the sentiment accordingly. This typically works on a graded scale from negative to positive, such as -5 to +5.

In the cases where customer comments reflect something extremely good, researchers can apply a highly positive tag to that and similar comments (+5). The same is true of the exact opposite (-5). In this way, entire language sets and taxonomies can be customised and evolved to the typical language a company might see, using the principles of Machine Learning.

TA and Sentiment Analysis results are typically visualised in interactive Dashboards very similar to those used in CX Platforms. These can include graphs, charts and cloud-based visuals such as Word Clouds and Sentiment Clouds.

Many CX Platform and surveying providers have developed TA applications that form a key part of their technology offers. Users do not necessarily acquire TA as a standalone product; it is very often incorporated into overall CX Platform solutions.

Alerts can be sent to individual users when particular trending sentiment increases or declines, or when keywords are mentioned.

Overall TA has become an extremely popular and highly effective method for CX professionals to conduct quantitative analysis on unstructured qualitative data and continues to aid advancements in CX research and management.

Also of interest: AI; Dashboard; Machine Learning; CX Platform; Manual Coding; Natural Language Processing; Sentiment Cloud; Sentiment Tag; Unstructured Data; Word Cloud.

TOP BOX SCORE
A method of examining only the top results from a set of research data, such as the top end of a graded scale or the top selection among answer options in a survey.

The purpose of this is to quantitatively identify how many respondents selected the top answer, and what top results "look like" based on customer comments.

Use of Top Box analysis can be applied to most research and survey response scales since only the top answers demand focus and attention from researchers. All other responses on the scale are ignored.

The logic behind this is to draw sole focus to the best results, therefore identifying the factors and features that make this possible. This approach also ensures that not all focus and investment is applied to the bottom end of response scales by attempting to address only the poor feedback results.

Top Box Scores can be reported as a percentage calculation based on the total number of responses collected. An example would be that if 20 respondents selected the top answer of a survey question (regardless of the scale used), and 100 respondents answered in total, the Top Box Score would simply be 20%.

Because Top Box Score analysis is used to focus only on the most positive elements of customer experience, this can be considered a limited view, as it does not enable varying respondent groups to be analysed and managed accordingly. It is therefore inadvisable that Top Box analysis be used as a means to manage a complete CX feedback programme which would also require customer dissatisfaction to be addressed and resolved.

Also of interest: Net Satisfaction; Net Score.

TOUCHPOINT
The specific moments of interaction between a company or service provider and its customers. Touchpoints are considered to be milestone events throughout a complete end-to-end customer journey.

Touchpoints are recognised as "key moments of truth" along a typical customer journey, as these specific engagement points might be the only times a customer has contact with the company from whom they have acquired products or services.

Many companies have entire operating models which are shaped around these moments of engagement with customers as there are, in theory, many potential touchpoints throughout a company-customer relationship lifecycle. An example from the automotive industry is as follows:
- Online browse
- Dealership visit
- Test Drive
- Finance review
- Order placement
- Order delivery
- Post-sale enquiry
- Servicing visit
- Sale or renewal

Since an understanding of typical customer touchpoints can be included within servicing and research design, they are used as ideal trigger points for CX surveying and feedback, forming an essential part of Closed Loop management processes.

Also of interest: Closed Loop; Journey Mapping.

TOUCHPOINT ANALYSIS
The analysis of information gathered at points of customer engagement known as "Touchpoints".

Also of interest: Touchpoint.

TRACKING STUDY
An ongoing, continuous research programme which tracks performance, results and survey outcomes over time. They provide a considerable advantage over single-wave or ad hoc research in that performance, perception and score changes across various periods can be analysed and understood.

Tracking studies are particularly useful in industries such as retail where customer buying behaviours and patterns can be measured across an annual period. They are also used in consumer Diary Tracking, where the effectiveness, use and impact of a product or service can be examined during a project window.

Typical Tracking Studies include the use of a key CX metric such as NPS or C-SAT, which is used to provide a score-based outcome at various points during the period of research.

TRANSACTIONAL NPS
Tactical NPS; tNPS
Net Promoter Score results that are collected from surveys which are sent right after a particular event, and ask about that event specifically, are known as transactional NPS surveys; often tNPS for short.

Use of tNPS is deliberately tactical, and the results shown from survey or research data collected in this way can often be unique. The reason for this is the transactional nature of the experiences being measured. Factors which drive tNPS can include:

- Specific events during overall experiences
- The behaviour of any staff members respondents come into contact with
- Emotive reactions
- Immediate impressions
- Direct comparison with other recent experiences

The wording of the NPS question itself should reflect an immediate or recent experience to capture feedback from the respondent only on that experience alone, such as:

"Based on the experience you had today how likely is it that you would recommend [this company, product or service] to a friend or colleague?"

Comparisons between tNPS and relationship NPS, also known as rNPS, can understandably be markedly different. This is because tNPS captures raw, immediate results based on a single recent event whilst rNPS asks respondents to recall their general impressions of a brand, company or service based on more than one experience over an extended period.

Also of interest: Net Promoter Score; Relationship NPS; Relationship Survey; Transactional Survey.

TRANSACTIONAL SURVEY

A research survey which is triggered by or follows a single customer purchase event very soon after the transaction has taken place. The nature of this type of customer interaction means that Transactional survey feedback is most relevant when collected very soon after the event to avoid the loss of event recollection.

Transactional surveys are typically very short questionnaires, focusing on the specific events of the recent experience, the customer's emotive reaction to those events, and can be underpinned by a CX feedback metric such as NPS or C-Sat.

The high volume of transactions between customers and companies means that automated software is often used to trigger Transactional survey invitations. Still, research methods can vary, and the following are some examples of use cases:

- Survey invite codes printed on customer till receipts following store purchases
- Web pop-up surveys triggered by the completion of online checkouts
- Exit Interviews conducted by onsite researchers following customer purchases

Different from Relationship-based surveys, which focus on customer feedback over time and many possible transactions, Transactional surveys focus only on feedback from single events. For this reason, they have become extremely popular in CX programmes worldwide as the high volume of data collected can be aggregated to enable an analysis of the drivers of customer satisfaction and loyalty. Many company CX strategies incorporate measurement of both Transactional and Relationship-based surveying to promote a balanced view of overall feedback and opinion.

Also of interest: Net Promoter Score; Relationship NPS; Relationship Survey; Transactional NPS.

TREND ANALYSIS
The examination of data over an extended period, so that data points may be tracked and compared to identify cause and effect, highlight the drivers behind changes and predict future results.

Trend analysis results are very often shown in a visual line graph format, where the X and Y axes may plot time vs score. Consequently, trend analysis is highly popular in CX research so that changes in data results can be examined and key drivers identified and understood.

TROUBLESHOOTING

The systematic approach to resolving service or product issues and problems as experienced by the customer or user. Troubleshooting involves a sequenced set of steps through which live agents, automated software or FAQs can help solve problems that prevent effective operation or usage. This is most commonly applicable to physical and electronic items such as computers, laptops, mobile phones, printers, etc. and software programmes.

Troubleshooting solution steps assume the problem or issue a customer is experiencing is attributable to a root cause. Therefore the sequence of resolutions will continue until no further suggestions can be made. It is at that point a recommendation can be made for the customer or user to talk to a specialised individual or seek an additional expert opinion.

U

UNSTRUCTURED DATA

Any data that is in a non-organised format, such as not having been grouped, categorised, defined, tagged or stored in any system of record or model.

Unstructured data is typically non-binary, non-numeric and non-quantified in any way. Written text is the primary and most commonly analysed form of unstructured data since languages of all kinds do not follow consistent formats or rules.

Analysis of unstructured data is growing rapidly, and many CX software companies have developed programmes and tools for mining meaning and sentiment from unstructured data sets such as:

- Customer verbatim in surveys
- Social Media chatter
- Customer-Agent chat dialogue
- Digitally transcribed audio
- Digitally transcribed video
- Digitally transcribed (or scanned) written content

The primary forms of analysis using unstructured data include tools which utilise Natural Language Processing (NLP) and Sentiment Analysis, both of which are provided by specialist software companies and used commonly in CX research.

Also of interest: Machine Learning; Natural Language Processing; Structured Data; Text Analytics.

UPTIME
The amount of time, usually measured in hours, days or as a percentage of total time, that a typical system or service is operating normally.

Systems measured using these statistics include hardware such as computers and laptops and software such as operating and CRM systems.

Optimal service uptime is typically expressed as 99.99%, where end-users may have experienced only minimal disruption to service throughout the measurable period. Consistently optimal service uptime is a component of positive CX, especially where customers and service representatives use online tools and applications, such as self-service banking and ordering systems.

USER EXPERIENCE
UX
A general term for the process of researching user interactions with solutions, services or products; typically websites, mobile applications, physical machines or devices.

Since UX focusses mainly on feedback based on functional activities, it is considered a sub-set of CX overall but does not fulfil the broader requirements of CX research. Therefore the two distinct terms of "UX" and "CX" are not synonymous and are mistakenly used interchangeably, which can cause confusion.

UX measurement collects a user's opinions and responses to the following:
- Features and functions (of a system such as a website or a physical machine)
- Simplicity and ease of use
- Time to achieve the desired outcome

- Clarity of information
- Impact on repeat and future usage

Because of the focus on a user's responses to elements such as design, layout, features and functions, UX mostly measures the effectiveness of self-service systems. Through examples such as those above, customers are increasingly able to engage with brands autonomously, not necessarily involving multiple human touchpoints along an extended experience journey.

For this reason, UX outcomes are considered particularly useful for product and service design teams, where direct feedback informs evolution. This can be important in areas such as automotive, website and mobile application development, which are now almost exclusively designed and redesigned based on critical rounds of UX feedback between version releases.

The formats of UX research methods can include Panel Groups, Community-based feedback, Diary-tracking, Surveys, Moderated and Unmoderated Observational Research, Web Analytics, Screen Heat Map Analysis, Eye Tracking and many more.

Overall, UX research forms an integral part of the research mix but does not exclusively answer or address all of the broader requirements of a complete CX strategy.

V

VARIABLE

A specific point of quantitative detail which will affect research outcomes, and can be any factor within the scope of measurement.

For example, a research survey which measures customer's experiences in a store would take into account what might vary during those experiences and affect the outcomes. These would be things such as the customers themselves, their age, gender, time and date of visit, visit purpose, etc.

In pure research, variables are classified in many ways, and two of these are used commonly in post-research analysis:
- Dependent variables: factors which are influenced by another variable
- Independent variables: factors which will change other variables

Using the example of customers visiting stores, the independent variables in this instance might be the layout of the store and the advertising used to attract customers to various offers. Meanwhile, the dependent variables might include a customer's responses to those factors in the form of how much they spent and their rating of the experience they had on the day.

In CX research it is important to understand how the linkage (if any exists) between independent and dependent variables affects customer experience the most, since controlling variables in certain ways can help influence customer opinion either positively or negatively. So feedback from customers who didn't respond positively to the layout of stores and the promotions on display can inform brands what they would need to change to influence customer spending and loyalty positively.

Also of interest: Attribute.

VERBATIM ANALYSIS
See: Text Analytics

VIDEO CX
An increasingly popular form of feedback in Voice of the Customer programmes, Video CX offers respondents the ability to record videos of themselves using device cameras whilst offering their thoughts and opinions on experiences they have recently had.

A link to the video survey can be embedded in the typical short-form survey a customer might receive after they have visited a location or had a brand experience. Upon clicking the link, they will be invited to complete a short video recording on their device, such as a laptop, mobile or tablet, using the front-facing camera (so they can see themselves whilst recording). The prompt before the video recording may be for the customer to answer a specific question, offer a general review of the visit or simply offer any experience-relevant commentary they wish.

This method of feedback combines the principles and benefits of ethnography, real-time data capture and emotive analytics in one. Videos can be used effectively within organisations to represent *actual* Voice of the Customer (whether shared as straight videos or transcribed and repurposed) or cut into shorter showreels to show different customer perspectives on a broad range of topics including services, products and brand reputations.

Video CX is a highly qualitative methodology which can enable customer interviewing at scale, but without the need for in-person researchers to conduct interviews in the field.

VOICE ANALYTICS
See: Speech Analytics

VOICE OF THE CUSTOMER
VoC
A general term describing the use of actual customer feedback and opinion within a CX research project or programme.

Many research projects can measure customer opinion and behaviour but without incorporating real commentary or feedback from customers themselves. Therefore VoC programmes and projects tend to include a higher proportion of qualitative data or verbatim captured directly from customers themselves, used to support quantitative findings.

An example of this is a scaled satisfaction question within a research questionnaire. Alone, that question would generate a score from the respondent, but unless accompanied by a following "Why did you choose that rating?" question, the reason behind the result has little context.

VoC puts more emphasis on storytelling and customer listening and has grown rapidly in popularity in recent years.

Additionally, VoC is commonly used within client companies as a name to describe the research programme itself, literally "The Voice of the Customer" programme, the use of which helps to affix an identity to the outcomes, rather than merely generically referring a set of CX results.

Also of interest: Customer Experience.

VOICE OF THE EMPLOYEE
See: Employee Experience

VOICE TRANSCRIPTION
Speech-to-Text; Voice-to-Text
The transcription of live dialogue, phone call conversations, sound files or any spoken and recorded materials into written text, usually for sharing, training or for analysis.

Voice transcription has been a capability offered by specialist companies for many years, where human agents would listen to spoken dialogue and transcribe this into written document form by manually typing or writing. The consequently written content would then be used for publication more widely, for providing training manuscripts for company employees or analysis by research firms based on the qualitative and emotive content.

The invention of speech-to-text software applications have made this task much easier in recent years, and many use the combined principles of Voice Recognition technology, Machine Learning and Natural Language Processing to transcribe words into text and conduct analysis on the content.

Voice transcription is used in CX to research and analyse customer calls and live dialogue, predominantly in Contact Centres, and then provide results analysis to assist in the management of customer experiences and expectations.

W

WEBCHAT
A form of live online message-based conversation between a representative of a company and a customer.
More recently, companies and service providers have begun to evolve and include VideoChat options.

Considered a vital channel for direct engagement with internet-enabled customers, many companies worldwide have chat capabilities built into their websites and mobile apps to facilitate customer issue resolution or to address general enquiries.

A new webchat is typically triggered through a customer clicking on a specific link or button to open up a new window, or by an agent monitoring a customer's activity on a website, proactively offering chat support to enable assistance.

The conversation takes place using a private 1 to 1 chat window which will pop up separate to the window the customer is using for their online browsing. This may include only text or a video option. Customer and agent then converse directly using messaging in the chat window. Once the chat has ended, a transcript of the entire conversation can be sent by email to the customer for reference purposes.

Many companies see the utilisation of webchat, alongside other customer engagement channels such as phone, email and face-to-face, as essential to a successful customer engagement strategy. For this reason, many companies also include a form of agent or service feedback rating or a link to a separate online survey following the conclusion of chats.

Also of interest: ChatBot.

WEB SURVEY
CAWI; Online Survey; Website Survey
A method of surveying research subjects where their responses are self-completed using online software.

Web surveys have gained in popularity since internet penetration has increased worldwide and have, in many instances, replaced former methods such as PAPI and CATI, both of which are typically more expensive and time-consuming to run.

This is mainly because the principle cost of PAPI and CATI research, i.e. research interviewers, are no longer required for self-completed web surveying. The survey software instead takes on the role of the researcher.

Respondents complete web surveys on their own using an internet-connected device such as a laptop computer, tablet or mobile. Web surveying is therefore generally more cost-efficient, scalable and adaptable than other research methods.

There are three main ways to provide access to web surveys for respondents, as follows:
- A unique link sent via an invite to a known target subject after an experience has taken place, typically triggered via an email or an SMS message. This is the more traditional CAWI (i.e. interview process) route
- A pop-up invite or intercept on the screen (computer or laptop) which is made available to any subject whilst browsing a website

- An always-on link which is available at any time for a subject to click on and access a web survey to provide feedback

In the above cases, the routing to the web survey questionnaire is different; hence the design of the survey will need to recognise the different respondent expectations to avoid a negative impact on completion rate. For example, a unique link sent to a respondent via email may carry more questions and the clear guidance of longer completion time. Meanwhile, a website pop-up survey should be short and relevant to the immediate experience the respondent has had.

A perceived drawback of web surveying is the much lower typical response rate compared with other more sample-focussed and interview-led research methods. These response rates can often be as low as single % figures based on outbound invites. This can often dissuade companies with smaller customer base sizes from undertaking web surveying as the insight which can be gained from low completion volumes is seen as unrepresentative and not worth the initial outlay and investment.

Meanwhile, for large enterprises who deal with thousands or millions of customers every day, a small % completion rate of web surveys may result in large numbers of feedback which is seen as a viable representative sample for ongoing analysis and experience management.

In today's CX market, web surveys are not only used as a method for data collection in the form of question-answer responses. The emphasis has shifted so that web surveys are seen as a critical touchpoint in initiating conversations with customers, triggered by the inclusion of Closed Loop questions within surveys, such as: *"Would you like someone to call you back about your issue?"* This has given rise to web surveys taking over as an essential research and engagement channel between many companies and their customers.

As a result, many CX strategies have been redeveloped to be built around continuous measurement using web surveying and trended reporting based on the insight gained from real-time data analysis.

For this reason, many CX software platform companies who offer continuous web surveying capabilities have gained many large customers and have significantly increased their revenues and growth in a period over the past ten years. These companies now specialise in survey design and production, data collection and analytics using results from web surveys.

Also of interest: Email-to-Web Survey.

WEIGHTED SCORE
Score weighting is a method of attributing a value to a single score or set of results based on its importance as part of an overall total.

In CX research, this method can be required when measurement using metrics or performance scorecards are made up of more than one set of results, and different "weights" need to be applied to each set. An example of a weighted score approach as may be seen in current CX programmes is as follows:

Overall CX scorecard:
- Online feedback survey scores = 25% of the total number
- Mystery Shopping results = 25%
- Telephone interview scores = 20%
- Face-to-face interviews = 15%
- Syndicated marketplace survey = 15%

In the example above, the results of customer feedback surveys and mystery shopping carry more weight as part of the overall CX scorecard. Meanwhile, although the other research methods in this example have less weighting, they also make up a % of the overall score.

Using a weighted approach such as this, companies managing CX strategies can balance the relative importance of different types of research as part of the overall mix. Many companies use this approach strategically, to ensure that employee focus will be on a specific set of measurable criteria whilst others are retained yet are de-prioritised.

Consequently, score weighting can assist with employee performance assessment, reward and recognition and measurement of goal achievement based on the weighting of CX factors as part of individual scorecards.

Also of interest: Scorecard.

WIDGET

A technology which allows sub-reports or mini data sets to be embedded in overall reporting suites such as online Dashboards. These are typically visualised as small individual windows on the main Dashboard, each showing a specific range of data, scores and reporting charts. Data included in each widget is typically pulled from a connected data source or uploaded content.

Many widgets make up the overall content of a Dashboard, and many software providers who enable Dashboard reporting give users a high degree of control over what each widget can contain and how the data can be represented.

Widgets are by their nature highly customisable and are therefore extremely useful for CX professionals who want to review and update research and data results in short visual form.

Also of interest: CX Platform; Dashboard.

WORD CLOUD

An automated software application which groups words and represents them in the image of a cloud or set shape. Word Clouds are used as a compact visual method of highlighting occurrence (and by association, importance) from unstructured data sets such as customer comments.

A Word Cloud is considered a quick and engaging way to reveal the most commonly mentioned phrases and words in a particular subject area and has seen much use in CX to highlight customer comments following experiences.

Word Clouds can be constructed based on the nature of the data sample (e.g. positive word cloud from positive customer comments vs negative). Sources of data in Word Clouds can be anywhere that written text is available and can be transposed into the Word Cloud software, such as from comments posted online, customer feedback from qualitative surveys, speech transcribed into text, and many more.

The methodology of data representation in Word Clouds, however, is not scientific and does not reveal anything more than how many times a word was mentioned or used in a sentence. The logic of Word Cloud software counts the number of times a word is included in the source sample and makes that word bigger or smaller in the resulting Cloud. Researchers using Word Clouds often have to work with source data for some time to filter out unnecessary conjunctions such as "a", "and" and "the".

The software is widely available on the internet for free, enabling users to upload data from source files such as Excel. Users have control over the colours, fonts, shapes and sizes of the Word Clouds themselves.

Also of interest: Sentiment Cloud.

WORD OF MOUTH

With origins in general language from the 1500s, "Word of Mouth" is used in CX to describe the personal opinions about a company, brand, product or service which a customer will pass on to someone else.

The term is used in CX very loosely and unscientifically as an indicator of brand advocacy. It is often used in situations where the results of CX research reveal that customers are likely to express either positive or negative word of mouth. It is a useful descriptor when discussing and highlighting advocacy drivers and the initiatives companies would need to undertake to improve positive customer ratings.

X

Hmm...nothing yet for the letter X. Except perhaps for the "X" in CX...?

Y

"Y" is this section empty...?

Z

"Zip" here...you are at the end of the book!

ACKNOWLEDGEMENTS AND REFERENCES

PROOFREADING ACKNOWLEDGEMENTS

I couldn't have completed this book without the proofreading critique and contributions of the highly professional international CXers with whom I am fortunate enough to be connected. There is a little piece of all of you within these pages. My thanks go to:

Sharon Boyd CCXP, Chief Customer Officer, MKL Innovation, UK

Christopher Brooks, Managing Director, Clientship, UK

Ruth Crowley CCXP, Vice President, Hudson Group, USA

Olga Guseva CCXP, Integria Consult, Russia

Nick Lygo-Baker CCXP, CEO, Paradigm CX, UK

A SPECIAL THANK YOU

...goes to my publisher **James Dodkins**, for supporting my efforts throughout the past year of writing, emails and calls back and forth, guidance and advice for my first solo publication, and for sharing my view that guitars look great hanging on the wall behind you on conference calls.

GENERAL RESEARCH RESOURCES

I have used a wide variety of general online and offline resources to construct definitions found in this book. The most commonly used were:

Google internet search
Wikipedia search
The Penguin English Dictionary, 2002 paperback edition

ABOUT THE AUTHOR

BEN PHILLIPS is a career Customer Experience professional, having worked in the industry since joining a Mystery Shopping company in 2006.

Since that first introduction to CX, Ben has worked in account management and leadership roles for surveying agencies, market research firms, a mobile technology service provider and client-side for a multi-national bank.

He became MRS certified in 2012 and a qualified CCXP in 2016.

Ben is now Global Head of Customer Experience for one of the world's largest research companies and travels and advises on CX measurement, methods, analysis, and management for companies across the globe.

He has co-authored two other titles and this is his first solo publication.

Before his career in CX, Ben worked in Customer Services roles for retailers, a pharmaceutical company and a confectionery sales business.

He was also a professional bass guitarist for a heavy rock band in the 2000s, touring the UK, France and Germany.

Ben's passions include recording instrumental jazz music at home, sampling from his extensive whisky collection and supporting Tottenham Hotspur FC.

FUTURE EDITIONS

For this edition of the CX Dictionary I had to make many decisions about what to include but also what to *exclude*. However, edition #1 is only the beginning. There is so much scope for more definitions, entries and guidance for people involved in the CX profession.

The Dictionary may grow to include new, updated and expanded entries in the future, creating an ongoing series of editions.

If you have any suggestions about future inclusions or would like to contribute an entry which you feel is important, please send your suggestions and ideas to:

thecxdictionary@gmail.com

I look forward to hearing from you.

Made in United States
North Haven, CT
02 December 2021

11871036R00143